AIR TO AIR

To Roy & Mary Lou—
Walt and I hope that
you enjoy my new book.

My very best,

Tim P Barew

Copy Editor: Ed Parrish

Book Consultant: Dave Franson

Creative Consultant: Gail Bowen

Design Consultant : Tony Blake

Tony Blake Design
1328 E. Kellogg Dr.
Wichita, KS 67211
(316)262-1333

Printed and bound in Japan by:

Dai Nippon Printing Co., Ltd.

For information contact:

Carey Schlosser

DNP America, Inc.

50 California Street, Suite 777
San Francisco, CA 94111
Tel: (415)788-1618
Fax: (415)495-4481

Library of Congress Catalog Card Number: 98-93073

ISBN 0-9665095-0-1

*Stock photography for use in advertising and promotional
materials available by written permission only. For availability
and pricing, contact:*
Paul Bowen Photography Inc.
(316)263-5537

To purchase a book directly:
1(800)697-2580

Distributed by:

NORTH SHORE PRESS

2300 E. Douglas
Wichita, KS 67214 USA

NORTH
SHORE

PRESS

AIR TO AIR

Photography By Paul Bowen

Foreword By Arnold Palmer

FOREWORD

I take great pleasure in contributing the foreword to *Air to Air*, the definitive collection of Paul Bowen's stunning aircraft photographs.

I've been flying for more than four decades, and Paul has taken aviation-related pictures of me since the early 1980s. Many of us who love airplanes have come to know him as a professional and admire his work for its artistic quality and precision.

Obviously, flying is a big part of Paul's life.

Likewise, it's a big part of mine, and it has been since 1958 when I started taking flying lessons. By then I'd begun winning on the tour, and my daughters had been born. While making a living was important, I was looking for a way to reduce the time I was spending away from my family, and that meant avoiding airlines and road trips.

Private aviation was really the only answer, and it proved a good one. Private airplanes are fast, they avoid traffic and terrain, they can land closer to most destinations than airliners can, and they reduce or eliminate the need for overnight stays.

Also, being a pilot is just plain fun.

Back when I was a regular airline passenger, traveling wore me out. Now that I'm my own pilot, flying energizes me. I invariably get out of the cockpit feeling refreshed.

The more I've flown, the more I've enjoyed it, the more necessary it is to me, and the more sophisticated my needs have become.

I bought my first aircraft, an Aero Commander 500, in 1961. A couple of years later, I had become so busy that I moved up to a 560F Commander and hired a part-time pilot to fly with me. Over the years, flying

became so essential to me and my business interests that I continued to buy faster aircraft with increased range and more versatile capabilities. I even flew an MD500 helicopter for a while. Thanks to my airplanes and to having the excellent and modern Westmoreland County Airport close to my

home in Latrobe, Pennsylvania, I've accomplished more than twice as much in my golf and business careers as I'd have been able to do with lesser means of transportation.

I'm not alone in this assertion. Business jets have become essential tools throughout the global village, and today's airplanes are better and safer than ever.

My own first jet was a Jet Commander in 1966. It opened up a whole new range of speed and versatility. Since then

I've owned and flown a Learjet and five Citations including my current Citation X, the fastest corporate aircraft ever built.

Since I began flying them, jets have multiplied my productivity beyond my wildest dreams. They have turned trips that would have taken three days on the airlines into matters of a few hours. They have shrunk the world to a manageable size and have enabled me to get to several sites, all hundreds of miles apart, in a single day. They have let me go where I needed to be, fulfill my commitments, and then fly back to have dinner with my wife that same night.

I look back at 1955 when I started out on the pro tour, back when Winnie and I had to drive from tournament to tournament. In those days we lived in a trailer and towed it behind a car barely powerful enough to pull it. On some of the longer trips, particularly the ones in which we had to

Left to right: Jim Kandt, Dian Lacine, Billy, Tom Jenkins, Paul Bowen, Mike Scratwieser, Arnold Palmer, Winnie Palmer, Ken Gero, Dane Jenning, and Murry Grieve

cross the country, when I got into a tournament town I literally got out of the car and stepped onto the first tee. This is a big country, 3,000 miles across, and exhaustion didn't do my golf any good.

But now, more than 40 years later, I can cross the country in four hours and arrive refreshed.

Back in the 50s, I certainly didn't foresee this capability. It's made Winnie's and my lives much more livable.

Paul's wife, Gail, has done us all a favor by supporting her husband's efforts and making it possible for him to go get these images. And Paul himself has done us a favor by assembling this collection of his favorites. He's letting us share the sights he sees through his lens.

Paul shows us today's most beautiful, high-tech sculptures. His views of these wonderful machines showcase their beauty and bring to mind the freedom they bestow upon the operators who guide them from point to point on our globe, a planet which they continue to make smaller and more accessible. He has been able to capture on film the thrill that we pilots feel each time we fly.

Best regards,
Arnold Palmer

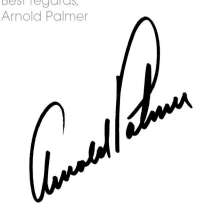

INTRODUCTION

It's safe to say that I have one of those dream jobs in aviation. I started shooting airplanes over 25 years ago and am among the fortunate few who shoot aerials for a living.

My first air-to-air shoot of a Beech Baron was also the first time I got airsick. Those of you who have tried aerial photography understand the challenges.

I have worked with many fine assistants over the years, including David Mann, Dick Yauk and Mike Fizer, the talented staff shooter for *AOPA Pilot* magazine. But, since 1988, my primary assistant, second photographer and loyal friend has been Tom Jenkins. He's shared long hours of cold assignments as we've toured the world together. The friendship that he and I have developed over the past 10 years is indicative of what you might expect working within the aviation community.

Tom and Paul at the Forbidden City - Beijing, China - 1998. Photo:Ed Parrish

I moved to Wichita from California in the early 70s after receiving my B.S. in Zoology from U.C. Santa Barbara. Through involvement in church sponsored street ministries in Hollywood during the late 60s, I accepted a position to direct a halfway house/crash pad in Wichita, Kansas. The

Reverend Don Schroeder at the First Presbyterian Church in Wichita brought me to Kansas. I loved the homemade desserts, the people, and their acceptance of me, long hair, long beard, and all. After directing the "Sonlight House" for one year I was encouraged by three families to remain in Wichita: Cessna Treasurer Bob Bauer and his wife Bucky; Cessna Public Relations Director Jerry Kell and his wife Betty; and Pat and Betty

Rowley. Pat owned an advertising agency that was responsible for producing Cessna's product brochures. He introduced me to the photographer who shot for Cessna, and I assisted him for $1.75 per hour. Six months later I was on my own as a free-lance photographer.

Paul and Dick Yauk in the tail of "Betty Grable" aka "Photo Fanny."
Photo:Mark Carter

It was on my first aerial photo mission that I realized how disorienting air-to-air shooting can be as you maneuver in formation while looking through a camera lens. That was the first and last time I was airsick. I decided that aviation photography, even with all of its challenges, was what I wanted to specialize in.

When my friend Molly O'Shaughnessy helped us out at the studio for a few months, she laughed at how often I would scribble "NICE GUY" next to an order I would take for one of our posters. I explained to her that most of the people in aviation are "NICE GUYS." When she stopped working in the studio, she presented me with a self-inking stamp. I use it daily.

NICE GUY

I have worked with most of the airframe manufacturers and their advertising agencies creating countless brochures and ad campaigns. I also have been credited with over 400 magazine covers. But you have to recognize that producing these photos is a team effort. The goal of this book is to present to you some of the teams and a sampling of the results from numerous shoots. Hopefully, through the group photos, you can share in the experience of THE TEAM. As I review my files, they conjure up wonderful memories of special friends.

THE PILOTS

The pilots are the true heros of this book and any aerial photo mission. Many of the outstanding formation pilots I know will be featured throughout the book. But a few long-term relationships need to be mentoned up front. Although I had flown numerous air-to-air sorties in various platforms,

Frank Tallman dazzles Citation crew members: Pilot Dick Thorndyke, Vice President Ogilvy & Mather Bob Rossitor, Pilot Bob Fizer, and Pilot Bill Hosmer. Tallman died shortly afterward in a plane crash.

my first B-25 shoot came in the mid seventies. TallMantz Aviation, named after famed aviation movie pioneers Frank Tallman and Paul Mantz, supplied the bomber. Chief Pilot Frank Pine supplied the talent. My professional admiration and friendship for Frank grew through the years as we shared sunrise after sunset. Frank's younger brother, retired Air Force Colonel Walter Pine, joined in as copilot a few years later.

Frank's death in 1984 was a great personal and professional loss to me. In recent years I've continued to work with Walt,

Walt Pine, Paul, Wayne Burtt, and Frank Pine (l.to r.) in final briefing.

The model 36 Bonanza is often used as a platform. Note the tail mounted Canon 35mm camera used for head on shots of the subject.
photo:Tom Jenkins

Kevin Eldridge, Steve Hinton and John Maloney using *Photo Fanny* (a.k.a. *Betty Grable*), the B-25 based at the Planes of Fame Air Museum in Chino, California. I'm thankful for the deep friendship Walt, his wife, Marilyn, and my family have developed. As a caring member of his Catholic Church and community, Walt is a living example of a quality life. I can think of no one I respect more.

Earle Boyter and I worked closely for many years producing advertising materials for Piper. He was not only the Director of Advertising and Marketing, but the primary formation pilot. When we went on location we worked hard and played hard. Piper's advertising agency was Group 3hree in Pompano Beach, Florida. Phil, Lee and David Rushlow produced award-winning literature for Piper. David's creative flair and innovative eye pushed my talents and helped me grow and mature in my craft. Earle and David are as close to me as brothers.

ADVERTISING AGENCIES

Cessna has been a client since the mid 70s. The group photos in the book well represent my friends at Cessna. Cessna's project director Tom Zwemke, and Sullivan Higdon & Sink advertising agency's Senior Art Director Jeff Filby, asked if I could get a new and improved variation on a shot I had previously achieved - "The Vorticies Shot." It was during a December shoot in 1991 that I shot the Citation coming through the fog causing the vortices to be revealed. The conditions were right, the lighting perfect, and through the skill of pilots Ben Budzowski and Will Dirks, we achieved the shot. In February 1992, Vice President of Marketing Phil Michel released the photo to *Flying* magazine. It became the most requested *Flying* cover photo ever. A poster followed. It still pleases me to see it displayed in offices and homes worldwide.

When Ralph Aceti joined Cessna's advertising team in 1979 he spearheaded new projects including the creation of Cessna's in-house *Directions* magazine. In an artistic layout, it features Citation operators based around the globe.

Stories about their companies and how they use their Citations as business tools created a communication device that appealed to CEOs and chief pilots. John Ross edited and wrote most of the articles. A retired journalist and pilot, John and I traveled the world together. His encouragement and desire to help me develop as a journalistic shooter helped me hone my craft even further. Most importantly, his guidance and listening ear were invaluable. John was followed by editor Nita Scrivner and currently by my close friend Ed Parrish.

While traveling with John, Nita and Ed, I was able to see the people of the world. To this day, I retain a special friendship with three unique and successful men - Felix Maguire of Anchorage, Capt. Rolim Amaro of Brazil, and Saad Wallan of Saudi Arabia. All three men share a passion for life and a masculine sensitivity for situations and people around them.

Felix Maguire is the Captain of a Citation V based in Anchorage, and owned by AT&T. In 1998 he became President of the Alaska Airman's Association. His career spans decades of flying various craft in extreme weather conditions. Landing and taking off in what most pilots would consider marginal situations has become commonplace to Felix. But, he doesn't take chances. He knows his equipment and his experience level. Behind Felix the aviator, is Deacon

Paul and John Ross on assignment in Beijing.

Maguire, an ordained Catholic Deacon. He holds services, directs community programs that really work for the local people, and has one of the greatest Irish smiles you'll ever encounter. Gail and I have spent time with Felix and his wife, Agnes, in Alaska, and are treated by surprise visits when he comes to Cessna or FlightSafety in Wichita. Our kids love to hear Felix's stories.

Rolim sent me letters of encouragement and comfort during my divorce. He shared some Brazilian wisdom that I refer to regularly. When we meet each year at the National Business Aircraft Association's convention, I remember that distance is no barrier to friendship. His "thumbs up" OK endorsing my new bride Gail, confirms his good taste in women.

Saad Wallan is a "rags to riches" success story. As the largest auto and truck dealer in Saudi Arabia, among many other business ventures, he was host to Tom Jenkins, Ed

Felix is at home whether in the left seat of the Citation, or on the business end of a salmon. The wide angle lens helped the catch.

Parrish, and me in Riyadh. His warm smile and hospitality were immediate and unbridled. We shared a commonality in our love and dedication to our children. When my father died of cancer in 1996, Gail, our kids and I went to California for the memorial service. Saad called me from Saudi Arabia to share his condolences and offer an ear if I needed a friend to just be there and listen. I was reminded again that friendship is not bound by time or distance.

AVIATION MAGAZINES

Shooting for a magazine article differs greatly from an advertising assignment. As an actor uses his talents for a television show or a movie, the approach, budget, time allotted to shoot, and advanced pre-production vary greatly. The same is true with magazine versus advertising shoots.

Rolim relaxes for the weekend at his cattle ranch in Brazil. His many interests include the breeding of Andalusian horses.

Saad serves tea at an outing he arranged in the desert outside Riyadh. The perfect host, no matter what the conditions.

This wonderful face belongs to a farmer in Brazil who appeared when he heard the engines start.

The eyes of this elderly woman captivated me as she strung chili peppers into a Santa Fe ristra.

CANON CAMERAS

In 1995 Canon Cameras amassed a group of 55 photographers whom they considered to be the best in their specialties. Mike Fizer and I were asked to join this elite group of professionals. I was further honored by having one of my Hawker 800XP aerials featured as the first ad in a new series featuring photographers and their work. Making dear Canon friends of Michael Newler and Dave Metz was a quality bonus to the contract.

These young Chinese soldiers pose for their picture to be taken on The Great Wall. The "classic rabbit ears" reminds us that people are very much the same the world over.

A normal studio staff meeting gathered around the "conference table." l.to r. Our Brazilian buddy, Tom, Heather Smith, Brian Cozine, Gail and Paul.

I have regularly contributed to *Aero* (Brazil), *A/C FLYER*, *BCA*, *Flight Training, Flying,* and *Twin & Turbine*. I have had the pleasure of getting to know great writers like Mac McClellan, Dick Collins, Tom Benneson, Scott Spangler, Mark Twombly, Kirby Harrison, Perry Bradley and Fred George, aka "Uncle Fred" to my children. Gail and I have been guests in Fred's home as well as close friends Jessica Salerno (*BCA*) and husband Jim Swickard. When Gail and I visit the annual NBAA convention each fall, the show becomes a reunion. We realize how "inbred" the industry is as we look closely at name tags to see "who's on first." For us, and many of you, that's part of the fun of our passion, aviation. We run into friends from all over the world.

By now you realize that I could have named this book "Plane Friends." Gail wisely counseled me to reconsider. To develop deep and lasting friendships while "in the trenches" has been an incredible experience.

I get plenty of compliments on my photography, and I appreciate that. But anyone who has been on a photo shoot will agree that the real credit goes to the entire team: the ad agencies and their art directors, the magazines, the manufacturer's advertising departments and mostly the pilots.

Finally, my most sincere thanks to Arnold Palmer for contributing the foreword. He embodies all that is good about family, competition, and aviation.

Here's to THE GREAT ADVENTURE!

To Gail: THE LOVE OF MY LIFE.
Who brought desire, trust and laughter back into my life.
I will love you forever!

CONTENTS

Heavy Iron

1

CHALLENGER 601-3R

The Canadair Challenger is one of a handful of corporate jets classified as "wide-body". Initially designed by aviation great Bill Lear, it is currently being built in Montreal, Canada, by Bombardier Aerospace. When it came time for an aerial photo session, we headed for southwestern United States.

California and Arizona are my favorite destinations because the weather is generally predictable, and a large variety of backgrounds are available. The B-25 photo platform is based in Chino, California.

For this project I worked closely with Larry Dionne, creative director of L.A.D. Communications in Montreal, to achieve the images needed for a new product brochure and ad campaign. We planned our schedule around weather, backgrounds, and of course, where we wanted to have dinner that evening.

Ground level, left to right: Pilot Nick Venn, Pilot Pete Newton, Director of Advertising and Promotions Bombardier Aerospace Business Aircraft Steve Phillips, Photographer/Assistant Tom Jenkins, Supervisor Photographic Services Bombardier Aerospace Garth Dingman, and Paul In B-25: Pilot Walt Pine, Pilot Kevin Eldridge, Creative Director L.A.D. Communications Larry Dionne, and Pilot/Mechanic Mark Foster

CHALLENGER 604

The B-25 is the best platform from which to shoot stills. When I'm sitting in the open tail-gunner's position I can move the trailing airplane quickly to achieve a variety of angles in a short amount of time. The intercom system within the B-25 allows me to communicate with my pilot. I tell him where I want the target moved and my pilot relays the message. Because I'm facing backward and can't see what is in front of me, I "filter" my directions through my pilot. When you're flying formation at 180 knots, things happen quickly. Safety is the most important issue.

Steve Phillips, director of advertising and promotions at Bombardier Aerospace Business Aircraft, directs Larry Dionne who creates the brochures and ads. Larry has the ability to design elegant pieces as well as pick the most lovely photos. I always know that I will get portfolio samples when I work with Steve and Larry.

Left to right: Larry Dionne, Pilot Geoff Foster, Steve Phillips, Pilot/Mechanic Jerry Wilkins, Supervisor Photographic Services Bombardier Aerospace Garth Dingman, Pilot John Maloney, Pilot John Race, Pilots Andrea and Kevin Eldridge, Photographer/Assistant Tom Jenkins, Linda Liscom, Pilot Ed Power, and as usual, Paul is in the tail position

A group photo is usually taken when on a location assignment. Here the crew poses at the Nut Tree Airport in northern California. Ed Power, pictured above with his wife Linda, owned the fine Nut Tree restaurant and gift store, featuring the excellent aviation section "One Flight Up."

CHALLENGER 604

I was called to shoot a quick aerial session for Challenger Public Relations Director Leo Knaapen. The National Business Aircraft Association was going to hold its annual convention in Las Vegas, and Leo wanted some pre-convention press photos of the then-new Challenger 604 flying over Lake Mead, located on the outskirts of Vegas. Famed test pilot Doug Adkins flew the 604. We shot from a Beech model 58 Baron with the doors removed. As we circled around the lake, we were treated to a beautiful sunrise and air-show-quality flying.

Doug Adkins poses in front of the Bombardier Flight Test Center in Wichita, Kansas.

CANADAIR SE

The Canadair Special Edition is a corporate version of Bombardier's successful commuter, the Regional Jet. As an interim airplane, prior to certification of the Global Express, the SE offered corporations the luxury of an extended cabin compared to the Challenger. I was able to team up again with my Bombardier pilot friends John Race and John Schutz as they took a break from their normal corporate flying.

We found ourselves shooting at my favorite lake, Lake Powell. Glen Canyon Dam retards the Colorado River on its journey southwest to the Grand Canyon. The dam is located in northern Arizona, but most of the huge lake sprawls into Utah. The contrast of blue water with red rock formations creates a wonderful background.

Left to right: Creative Director L.A.D. Communications Larry Dionne, Pilot Kevin Eldridge, Pilot Alain Lacharite, Pilot John Schutz, Pilot John Race, Paul, Pilot/Mechanic Matt Nightengale, Pilot John Maloney, Supervisor Photographic Services Bombardier Aerospace Garth Dingman, Photographer/Assistant Tom Jenkins, Pilot/Mechanic Rick McCoy, and Photographer Lucio Anodel
Photo by: Garth Dingman

GLOBAL EXPRESS

The Global Express is gorgeous. When you first see it, you're impressed by its beauty. As you get closer, you become even more impressed by its size. The attention to detail is consistent with the quality you would expect in this category of airplane.

Corporate travelers aboard the Global Express can cover distances never before available, non-stop, and in total comfort. You can see the Global Express interior on pages 204-205.

Left to right: Paul, Pilot Ronnie Gardner, Marketing Coordinator Nancy Smoot, Flight Test Engineer Matt Wologwyn, Pilot Ralph Royce, Photo Assistant Nate Bunck, and Pilot T.C. Jones
Not pictured: Global Express Pilots Pete Reynolds, Ron Haughton, Bruce Robinson, and Peter Boyd

EMBRAER EMB-145

The Brazilian-built Embraer EMB-145 was on a demo tour when I caught up with it in Palm Springs, California. My father had recently died and my family and I were in California for the memorial service. I agreed to fit in the shoot between family commitments.

Davo Dickerson from Kootin, Rich & Dickerson Advertising Agency, coordinated the session as we shot ground exteriors and interiors in the morning. *Business and Commercial Aviation* magazine sent Senior Editor Fred George to cover the event for an article. All this was followed by an afternoon aerial session to Catalina Island. Piloting the EMB-145 were Embraer Test Pilots Madureira and Gualda. My Planes of Fame friends supplied the B-25, and we had a lovely evening.

AIR CANADA

I arrived late in the morning at Clay Lacy's FBO in Van Nuys to brief for the afternoon shoot. The client was Air Canada, which needed its new Airbus 340 shot in both motion and stills. Clay is the consummate professional. He choreographs his Learjet around the subject plane, while the camera operator rolls film through an elaborate periscope system mounted in the belly and top of the fuselage. The still shooter works primarily through the windows.

The 340 was coming from Toronto. It would rendezvous in flight, work with us for about an hour and a half, and then break off without landing and return to Toronto, non-stop. To accomplish this legally, it required two flight crews on board. The pilots briefed on the phone and off we went. We flew up to northern California chasing mountains and clouds. Clay and the Lear made my job easy.

The shadow Clay's Learjet cast on the Airbus gives you an idea of relative size. When shooting aerials, you must watch for the platform airplane's shadow ruining the shot. Look closely in magazines and you will see that mistake periodically. In a rush to get printed, details sometimes get over-looked.

The group photo, left to right: Copilot Scott Patterson, Art Director Steve Crawford from Marketel Advertising in Montreal, Assistant Cameraman Darin Necessary, Astrovision System Operator Doug Allen, and Clay

FALCON JET

Organizing a major photo shoot can be incredibly difficult. This is especially true when you gather four target planes and a platform together. John House scheduled to take a Falcon 100, 200, 50, and 900 to the red rock area of Arizona.

Days before the departure date, Art Scholl, famed aerobatic and motion picture stunt pilot, was killed while filming the movie *Top Gun*. His death touched many lives. A memorial service fly-by was scheduled at his airport the day our shoot was to begin. We coordinated our B-25's departure so we could be the lead ship in the ceremony. As we passed by the crowd, we banked left, and headed for Monument Valley, Arizona.

This shot was taken at Lake Powell in September, 1985.
Left to right: Jean-Marie Barthelemy, Jim Meyer, Bob Johnson, Ron Standerfer, Mark Russo, John House, Paul, Bob Healy, Fred Westeraberg, Ed Allen, Walt Pine, Herve Leprince-Ringuet, Steve Hinton, Jan Williams, John Hinton, Jim Oakes, Randy Kennedy, Chris Thompson and Rod Foster

Falcon 900

The VFR corridor down the Hudson River allows you to fly by the Manhattan skyline and look up at the impressive buildings. This area can be busy with sightseeing smaller planes or helicopters. When you introduce a formation flight with a high performance corporate jet flying in slow formation, it further complicates everything. Ed Allen, director of flight for Falcon Jet, flew the excellent formation, with copilot Rich Iudice.

After passing by the Trade Towers a few times, we departed the area to catch the sunset above a cloud bank to the west. I was shooting through the open pilot's window of a Cessna 210. My hands still hurt when I think how the cold wind cut through the gloves and ski mask I wore.

FALCON JET

It is always difficult to make a large formation look good in a photograph. The pilots may be flying in precisely the right position for normal formation work, but from the camera's position, they may not look lined up. Through radio communication with the target planes, I constantly jockey them up, down, forward, and backward slightly.

This all changes when the airplane to be photographed is in the formation lead. Then I fly "off them". I tell my pilot to maneuver up and down as needed for the best photograph as the subject airplane holds a steady course.

But when you have five airplanes flying in close formation, the scenario gets more complicated. Everyone is constantly changing position per my direction. Obviously, it takes talented and experienced pilots to fly safely and get the necessary photos. These Falcon pilots had lots of formation experience and the photos show it.

Left to right: Pilots Jerry Tritt, Chuck Tennstedt, Ken Dromgold, Bob Kane, Rich Iudice, Guy Mitaux-Maurouard, Harry Shepard (pilot and owner of the Marchetti), Dave DeAngelis, Ed Allen and Paul
Not pictured: Director John House

GULFSTREAM IV-SP

This photo shoot was scheduled for the west coast during February of 1998. We had an agenda planned for weeks. El Niño had other plans. We grouped and regrouped for three days, dodging weather bullets as we changed destinations in flight. The results were worth the effort. Anderson Communications Group's art director Donna Thomas and producer Stacey Berndt were troopers as they helped us decide where to go for the best images for their client's Gulfstream. This was a great example of how the team can work together and how important it is to work with professionals.

Left to right: Pilot Kent Crenshaw, Mechanic Plato Smith, Pilot/Mechanic John Hinton, Pilot John Maloney, Pilot Randy Gaston, Steven Hinton, Pilot Steve Hinton, Art Director Donna Thomas, Account Executive/Producer Stacey Berndt, Advertising Director Greg Goyne, Photograher/Assistant Tom Jenkins, and Paul

GULFSTREAM V

My first photo session with the Gulfstream V took place during the certification process while the airplane still had the probe on the nose and explosive parachute in the tail cone. The advertising agency would "retouch out" these undesirables, but I left them for you to see.

Ralph Aceti was then vice president of marketing for Gulfstream. I had worked with Ralph through his years with Citation, Challenger, Learjet and now Gulfstream. I respected his advertising savvy and appreciated being able to carry our friendship once again into the business arena. Currently he is President of ClearView Marketing & Communications, an aviation related business based in Hilton Head, South Carolina.

We headed east, chasing clouds at sunrise. Before we knew it, we were miles off the coast. If I had stopped to think about being in a B-25 that was built before I was born, I might have become uneasy. Fortunately, Ralph Royce at the Lone Star Flight Museum keeps his planes in top condition. We accomplished the shoot without a hiccup.

This gaggle includes B-25 crew: Billy Parker, Ralph Royce and T.C. Jones
Camera crew: Video Cameraman John Funchess,
Photographer/Assistant Tom Jenkins, and Paul
Various Gulfstream personnel joined in for the photo

Gulfstream V

The G-V has an incredible family tradition. Gulfstream's success is unparalleled in corporate aviation. The Savannah-built aircraft has earned a reputation in the business community for quality, reliability, performance and continues to command a loyal and vocal following. There was no difficulty in finding flattering angles to shoot this long-range workhorse.

Standing left to right: Pilot Kevin Eldridge, Producer Joe Bergeron, Pilot Jim Keller, Pilot Hank Gibson, Pilot Ted Mendenhall, Technician Tony Newbold, and Technician Dean Hunter
Kneeling: Video Photographer John Funchess, Pilot/Mechanic John Hinton, Pilot John Maloney, Photographer/Assistant Tom Jenkins, and Paul

UPS - Boeing 767

This shoot was the most elaborate and well organized event I have ever been associated with. UPS primarily wanted footage for television commercials to be used during the Olympic Games through the year 2000. As the still photographer, I was the stepchild.

UPS provided two 767-300ERs for the weekend. Saturday was dedicated to shooting aerials. On Sunday we shot beauty shots, takeoffs, and landings. Stan McClain, president of the Society of Operating Cameramen, shot the air-to-air using Wolfe Air's Learjet featuring the VectorVision periscope system. Jeff Senour piloted the Learjet as we danced around the heavy iron. Jeff and I had flown together before, so my comfort level was very high.

Ammirati Puris Lintas advertising agency in New York hired Steve Ross of Venus Productions in Venice, California, to produce the event. Steve was responsible for the meticulous organization. We all knew our responsibilities and where we were supposed to be at any given time. Director Jim Sonzero choreographed both the aerials and ground shooting. As expected, the results were stunning.

Above: Cinematographer Stan McClain discusses the shot list with Director Jim Sonzero.
Gathered around the Learjet, left to right: Assistant Cameraman/ Technician Kent Hughes, Cinematographer Stan McClain, Director Jim Sonzero, Copilot Christian Falco, Pilot Jeff Senour, and Paul
Not pictured: 767 Pilots Paul Aubrey, Lance Stephenson, Jay Barnes, and John Fanning

UPS - Boeing 767

Two movie crews came for the ground shots. Stan McClain took air-to-ground shots from Helinet's Bell Jet Ranger piloted by Rick Shuster. Veteran Cinematographer Thomas Kloss took all the ground shots.

We worked at the Southern California International Airport, formerly George Air Force Base, in Victorville, California. This was the first time I had shot a 767 doing a touch-and-go. I knelt on the runway to get a near head-on shot. On the first pass, the wind blast from the 767 blew me over. I grabbed my two sturdy tripods and cameras on my way down saving the long lenses from damage. I brushed myself off, looked around to see who might have been watching, and pretended I had meant to do that.

A group gathers to watch the video monitor: Director Jim Sonzero, Print Art Director Lona Walburn, Ammirati Puris Lintas Producer Bob Shriber, UPS Vice President Customer Communication Paul Meyer, and Producer Steve Ross.
Touch and go landings and takeoffs continued through the day.
The 2 photos above were shot by Joel Costello.

2

MID-SIZE
CORPORATE JETS

CITATION III

I have shot the Cessna Citation 650 series since the Citation III's first-flight takeoff. One of my early sessions with the III took me out to California. We flew around Big Bear Lake near Los Angeles, then up the coast to northern California. When we reached Monterey, we found fog around the coastal mountains.

Frank Pine and his brother Walt crewed the B-25 out of TallMantz Aviation at John Wayne Airport in southern California. Ralph Aceti headed the advertising for Citation directing the art director from Ogilvy Mather advertising agency, Chicago. This was one of the early shoots in my career that allowed me to work with quality professionals. Assignments like this helped me stretch my creativity.

Ground level, left to right: Paul, Pilot Jim Lapine, Pilot Walt Pine, Pilot Bob Fizer, Camerman Jack Cooperman, and Pilot Frank Pine

On the B-25: Advertising Director Ralph Aceti, Mechanic Wayne Burtt, Camerman Wayne Baker, Art Director Rich Adkins, and Photo Assistant Mike Newby

CITATION III

I first met Lee Lauderback when he was chief pilot for Arnold Palmer. Arnie was then flying a Citation III and a Hughes 500 Helicopter. I was on an assignment for Cessna's *Directions* magazine. Ann Williams, director of marketing communications at Cessna, interviewed Arnold for her article while I shot photos. We hopped into his helicopter, with Palmer at the controls, and flew from his Bay Hill Country Club to the then-under construction, Isleworth Country Club - both located in Orlando, Florida, where Arnie lives during the winter months. I must say that "The Boss" as he is referred to by Lee, is one of the most gracious and consistently nice people I have ever met. He talked to the construction workers by name, and probably made them feel that they were the most important people he would see that day. No wonder "Arnie's Army" continues to grow.

Later that day, I shot an air-to-air session with Lee at the controls. His son, Brad, now an adult and a pilot, rode along in the Citation. Brad can be seen peering over his dad's shoulder. Lee now owns Stallion 51 Corp., and flies a dual control TF-51 Mustang (pages 160-161).

Lee Lauderback and son Brad fly together in their sailplane. Standing: Citation Copilot Lance Long and Paul

CITATION VII

This shoot was a turning point in my career. Even though I had been shooting aerials for twenty years, I didn't have a "signature" shot. That ended with this shoot.

Tom Zwemke, director of corporate communications at Cessna, and Jeff Filby, senior art director at Sullivan Higdon & Sink advertising agency, directed a video and still shoot in California. Clay Lacy provided his Lear for the video, and Aero Traders from Chino, California, supplied the B-25.

This large group consists of Aero Traders pilots and the still photography crew, Clay Lacy's movie crew, and the Citation pilots and advertising personnel

After spending the night in Reno, Nevada, we popped over the mountains to shoot Lake Tahoe at sunrise. Fogged in, the lake provided the perfect conditions to recreate and improve upon a vortices shot we had shot once before.

Phil Michel, vice president of marketing at Cessna, released the image to *Flying* magazine. It became the most commented upon cover ever to appear on the magazine.

B-25s use so much oil that *Pacific Princess* carries its own supply.
Left to right: Paul, Tom, Senior Art Director Jeff Filby, Pilot Tony Ritzman, Pilot Carl Scholl, and Pilot/Mechanic Richard Reed

CITATION EXCEL

The Excel was a marketing success even before it was built. By the time it was certified in April 1998, over 200 orders had been placed. The eight-passenger jet can be categorized as a mid-size, or a light jet. It is a combination of the Citation Ultra and Citation X. It's the first aircraft to combine light-jet performance with a stand-up cabin.

I first photographed this new model over the cloudy skies of Kansas. Cessna's Director of Corporate Communications Tom Zwemke came along to shoot video.

The certification process is so deadline driven, an experimental airplane is only available for short periods of time for photo sessions. We had one shot at it. Fortunately, the clouds gave us an interesting background. I used a fisheye lens to achieve the high-altitude look in the picture below.

Tom Zwemke takes video footage through the open window area of this Cessna 210 Centurion. The custom designed windows are removable in flight on both sides of the airplane. The noise caused by the opening necessitates wearing a headset for ear protection and to communicate with the 210 pilot.

CITATION X

Tom Jenkins, my assistant/second photographer, shot the Mach .92 Citation X aerial for Jessica Salerno of *Business and Commercial Aviation* magazine who contacted us to shoot the airplane for a cover story. Tom shot the aerials through the cockpit and passenger windows of a CitationJet. To avoid reflections he wore black clothes and gloves and draped the pilots in black velvet. The only thing that upset me about his shoot was that I can't claim the striking images as mine. I do claim the ground shot of the 2,500th Citation. Ed Parrish, editor of Cessna's *Directions* magazine, and art director Shirley Harrold worked with me into the evening hours as we set up lights to shoot at the magic hour of dusk.

In a category by itself, the Collier Trophy-winning Citation X is the fastest corporate airplane currently in production. The coveted Collier Trophy recognizes companies and products for innovative design and safety. Cessna is the only general aviation manufacturer to receive the award twice.

LEARJET 60

I'm not a pilot, so I look at airplanes primarily as sculptures for me to photograph. Of course I love flying, but my job is to create exciting imagery, not to fly the plane.

I primarily shoot Canon EOS-1n 35mm cameras when in the air. The lenses are so sharp and the film is so good, that I get more variety in a short time without compromise to sharpness and reproductive quality. I take four camera bodies with me. My primary lenses are the 28mm-70mm zoom lens and the 70mm-200mm zoom lens. I also use my 17mm-35mm zoom and my 16mm fisheye. When the light gets low, I reach for my 85mm f1.2 lens. And recently, I have used Canon's new Image Stabilization (IS) lenses. Currently I have the 75mm-300mm IS zoom and the 300mm IS lens. The Image Stabilization acts like a gyro to dampen vibrations and motion. I used the 75mm-300mm IS lens to capture the cover image of this book.

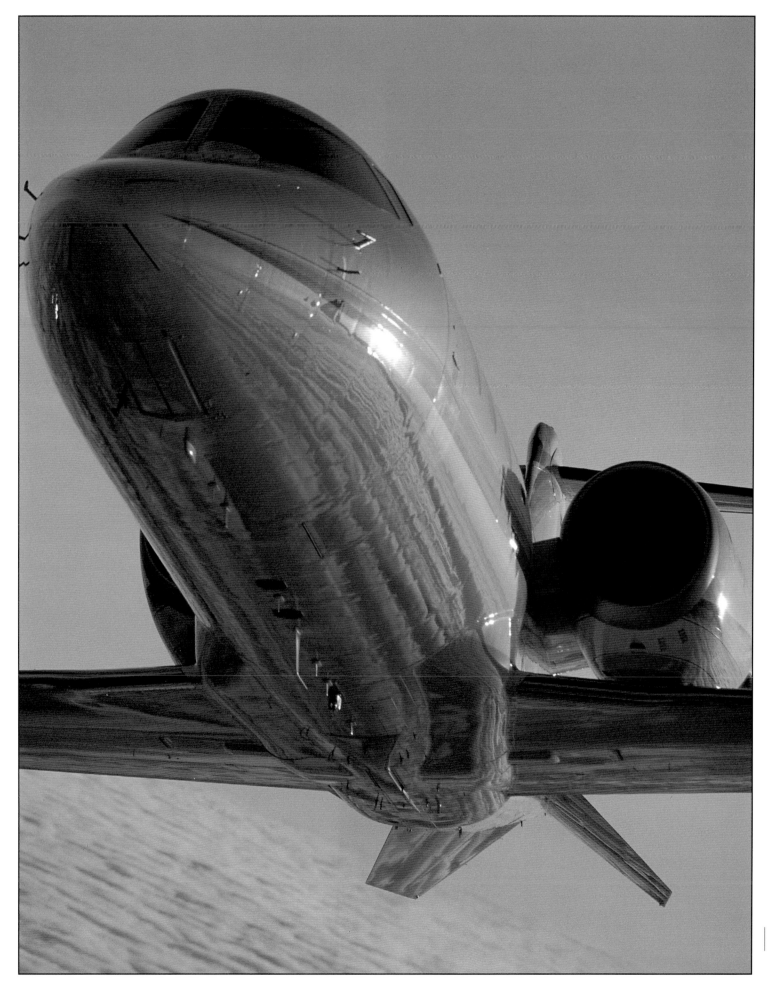

LEARJET 60

The Lear 60 is fast, spacious, and beautiful. When I heard pilots Bob Agostino and Dave Sullivan sincerely praising the virtues of the Lear 60, even I got excited. When we started flying it got better.

Learjet hired my wife, Gail, to assist me. My regular assistant, Tom Jenkins, was tied up at the studio sorting 160 rolls of film from the Lear 31A shoot we had done the previous week. Gail had never seen the "vortices" shot in action. We were working off the coast on top of the marine layer when we created these shots. In spite of the deafening roar of the B-25 with open tail cone and my David Clark headsets securely in place, I could hear Gail scream with delight as the vortices appeared. After the photo session, I recognized a unique opportunity. Gail and I were the only occupants in the back half of the B-25, so we became initiated into that *special club* to which pilots irreverently refer. We look back at that event and laugh and blush.

My manhood is only slightly threatened that there was only one scream of delight that morning.

Left to right: Supervisor Photographic Services Bombardier Aerospace Garth Dingman, Pilot Dave Sullivan, Pilot Bob Agostino, Pilot/Mechanic John Hinton, Sid and Terry Garrison, Gail, Paul, and Pilot Kevin Eldridge In cockpit: Pilot/Mechanic Matt Nightengale

The crate contains an antique Chinese herb cabinet Gail and Paul purchased in Chinatown San Francisco. It rode in the bomb bay during filming before resting in the isle of the Lear 60 on its way back to Wichita.

LEARJET 60

During the late 1990s many companies began programs for fractional ownership of airplanes.
Bombardier's is called Business Jet Solutions. One
of the airplanes included is the Learjet 60.
Fractional ownership has introduced individuals
and companies to the benefits of general aviation
travel, its safety, convenience, comfort, security,
flexibility and cost-and time-saving benefits. Once
you've spent any time in corporate aircraft, you
realize how important they are as business tools.

We chased the airplane early one morning, flying
north of San Francisco and slightly inland. The sky
was gorgeous as we shot from the nose of the B-
25. I used a tinted filter, similar to your car wind-
shield, to darken the sky and enhance the dawn's
warm colors.

Left to right: Pilot Sam Daniels, Photographer Garth Dingman, Pilot Gary
Krambs (friend of Paul's and Chief Pilot for F. Korbel and Bros., Inc - the
California Champagne, Wines, and Brandy Company), Paul, Pilot/
Mechanic John Hinton, Keri Orton, Pilots Kevin and Andrea Eldridge, and
Pilot Captain George Steven

LEARJET 45

The Lear 45 is already backordered for years. The excitement building around this newest addition to the Bombardier family of aircraft is contagious.

While the 45 was still in flight test, we took a painted prototype around the Kansas and Oklahoma skies. Jim Dwyer, manager of Learjet flight test programs, and copilot Steve Thompson, flew the 45. Ralph Royce and his gang from Gavelston brought their B-25 up for the shoot. Some summer morning build-ups helped break up the midwest landscape. Because we based out of Wichita, Gail was able to include her father, Don Hilton, on one of the sessions. I guess she thought it was good for him to see that I really had an actual job.

Left to right: Pilot T.C. Jones, Marketing Coordinator Nancy Smoot, Pilot Ronnie Gardner, Gail, Pilot Ralph Royce, Gail's father Don Hilton, Director of Advertising and Promotions Bombardier Aerospace Business Aircraft Steve Phillips, and Paul

Hawker 800XP

This was one of the most successful shoots ever. We covered the western half of the country as we sought and found beautiful backgrounds. We shot primarily from *Photo Fanny*, and a couple of days from a Beech Baron. The two aft side doors are removed and I sit backward in the center seats. Tom Jenkins, my assistant, sits next to me, reloads my cameras, and also shoots backup. The speed of the Baron, even with the doors removed, is compatible with the lower range of the Hawker.

Mono Lake is pictured on page 67. It is located in northern California, near Death Valley. Its unusually high mineral content causes crystaline formations to appear around the shoreline as the water evaporates.

Ground level left to right: Paul, Pilot Rob Jenner, Green Tree Financial Corporation's Chief Pilot Jon Paschka, Pilot John Maloney, Pilot Kevin Eldridge, and Pilot Walt Pine
In the B-25, left to right: Account Executive Tom Bertels, Manager Media and Promotions John Odegard, Art Director Steve Nelson, and Photograher/ Assistant Tom Jenkins

HAWKER 800XP

Vortices shots have become my trademark. When there is a marine layer off the California coast, it provides perfect conditions for these pictures. The pilots decide if the conditions are safe and obtain necessary clearances. We drop down into the layers and produce a variety of unpredictable images. Tom Jenkins and I are the only ones who get to see the performance until the film is processed. It is so exciting that sometimes I just want to put the camera down and enjoy the ballet. Lucky for you I never do.

It was on this assignment that I shot the cover photo and the Canon Camera ad pictured on page 9 in the introduction.

"The Happy Hawker"
Left to right: Photographer/Assistant Tom Jenkins, Pilot Todd Hanna, Pilot Rob Jenner, Pilot Jon Paschka, Manager Media and Promotions John Odegard, Art Director Steve Nelson, Paul, Pilot Greg McCurley, Pilot Marty Unrein, and Account Executive Tom Bertels

ASTRA

This shoot began in California with the B-25. We worked our way up the coast from Los Angeles, ending the two day session in San Francisco. The Golden Gate Bridge always works well as a back-drop as we wind our way over the bridge out to open sea and back around into the Bay over Alcatraz Island. Then we continue near the skyline and past the Oakland Bay Bridge.

At San Francisco we joined up with the WolfeAir Learjet and headed north toward Anchorage. Jeff Senour piloted the Lear with the finesse of a surgeon as he maneuvered around the two Astras. Just outside of Anchorage we noticed the plume of smoke coming from Mount Redoubt. We investigated and were rewarded with this spec-tacular shot.

Left to right: Cameraman Bob Vogt, Assistant Cameraman Mark Streapy, Photographer/Assistant Dick Yauk, Diane Jorgensen, Pilot Jeff Senour, Pilot Dick McNulty, Pilot Jim Deeth, Pilot Jim Brown, Pilot Don Majors, Creative Director Herb Clark, Pilot Duane Brown, and Paul

LIGHT JETS

3

LEARJET 25

This was one of my early jet shoots. The unique paint scheme on this Lear 25 worked well with many backgrounds. We constantly move the target ship around as we position it against the background. The light affects both the airplane and the background.

The subject airplane's pilot watches the lead airplane to maintain separation. The pilot jockeys the throttles back and forth to keep his airplane in position. It's very difficult work requiring strict concentration.

Through the years I continued to fly with Chet Eby. He never complained about the long hours. He always showed up on time. He always contributed more than was asked of him. There is no better pilot, no better man.

Standing left to right: Pilot Bill Perke, Mechanic Wayne Burtt, Pilot Frank Pine, Pilot Walt Pine, Pilot Rory Hanson, Pilot Pinky Jones, Pilot Chet Eby Kneeling: Learjet Public Relations Director John Meyer, and Paul

LEARJET 31A

This was my first vortices shot. Other variations have gained more notoriety and exposure, but this was the beginning. It actually came as a mistake. Art Director Susan Ash asked if I could get a shot of the Lear climbing out of the fog bank at a deck angle reminiscent of an F-16 going vertical. I explained that wasn't possible. We made an attempt, but before the Lear pilot could do a pull-up, Tom Jenkins and I were the only ones who could see the vortices being revealed behind the Lear. The images we took were so dramatic we abandoned the first idea.

Standing left to right: Pilot/Mechanic John Hinton, Pilot Kevin Eldridge, Paul, Pilot Chet Eby, and Pilot Walt Pine
Up front In the B-25: Account Executive Jon Cassatt
In the cockpit: Pilot Dick Sutter
On top: Photographer/Assistant Tom Jenkins

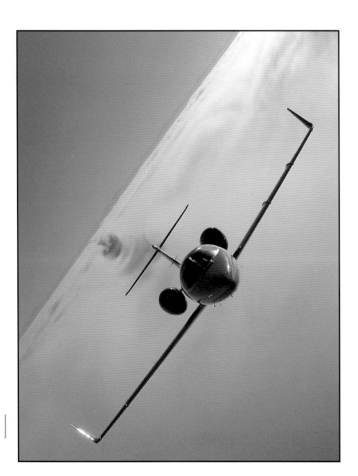

LEARJET 31A

When Learjet decided to attempt a speed record flight, public relations people called *Flying* magazine's Editor in Chief Mac McClellan and asked him if he would like to be the copilot and write an article about the flight.   We went to Aspen, Colorado, for the departure. Aspen to Washington, D.C. in record time was the goal.

Advertising Vice President Ralph Aceti and Public Relations Director Jeff Miller joined the crew to help record data. Learjet's Flight Test Engineer Kirk Vining recorded the official data. As pilot in command, Learjet's famed Chief Test Pilot Pete Reynolds, put it all together.

Fortunately for me, the pictures turned out.

Fortunately for Learjet, Pete set the record.

August 25, 1994, three hours, six minutes, 41 seconds.

The group posed in Aspen: Mac McClellan, Pete Reynolds, Kirk Vining, Ralph Aceti, Jeff Miller and Paul

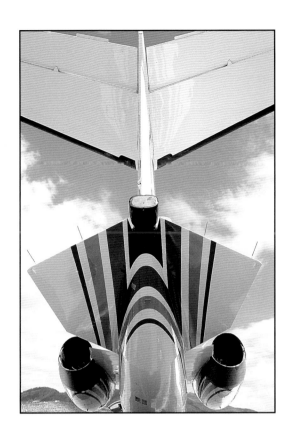

LEARJET 31A

This was an extra special mission. I love to photograph the Learjet product line. But what made this important to me was that I had chosen this flight and this set of friends to share in the spreading of my father's ashes. My brother Lance deposited half of the ashes where he lives in Hawaii. I had told my dad that my half would be spread between the Santa Barbara Channel Islands and the California coast - from the B-25.

After the morning photo session, I asked my friends in *Photo Fanny* to join me in remembrance as I spoke over the intercom. Tom shot a picture as I scattered the least important part of Lansford Dennison Bowen, a.k.a. Lance, from the back of the B-25. My special thanks to my friends for making that important time in my life more memorable.

Thank you Steve, Kevin, John, Steve, Garth and Tom.

The gang regrouped in Santa Barbara before heading north.
Left to right: Supervisor Photographic Services for Bombardier Garth Dingman, Pilot Dave Sullivan, Pilot Rod Lundy, Pilot Steve Hinton, Steven Hinton, Pilot/Mechanic John Hinton, Tom Jenkins kneeling, Pilot Kevin Eldridge, Director of Advertising and Promotions Bombardier Aerospace Business Aircraft Steve Phillips, Project Manager Sharon Core, Video Photographer Mike Rixon, and Paul

BEECHJET 400A

I've spent a lot of time flying with Beechjet pilots, but I've spent more time socializing with them. Roy Lawrence, Garvin Speed, Bob Brown, and Ed Berger have become close friends. It should be no surprise that we work hard when we shoot on location, but we attempt to counterbalance that with serious fun. Add people like Bill Condiff from Beech's advertising department and Bill Edwards with McCann-Erickson advertising agency, and you have the potential for great memories. This photo shoot was no letdown.

When we shoot from the B-25, we get shots of angles that can only be achieved shooting from the tail gunner's position. The extreme takeoff is a very difficult shot. Garvin Speed and Roy Lawrence have it down to an art form. Not to be outdone, Bob Brown has achieved nearly the same deck angle in a rental car as we became airborne over railroad tracks.

The *Pacific Princess*, based in Chino, is operated by Aero Traders. Left to right: Paul, Pilot/Mechanic Richard Reed, Pilot Carl Scholl, Pilot Tony Ritzman, Director of Advertising Bill Condiff, Pilot Bob Brown, Pilot Garvin Speed, Pilot Roy Lawrence, and Art Director Bill Edwards

Beechjet 400A

The same wild group pictured in the two previous pages was responsible for this two-page spread. We worked around the Santa Barbara Channel Islands off the California coast when I pulled out the fisheye lens. Although we were at a relatively low altitude, the fisheye gives the appearance of higher flight.

Years after Mt. St. Helen's eruption, the volcano's steam continues to remind us of nature's power.

You can't imagine how cold it can become flying around at altitude with doors off planes. The wind chill can be debilitating sometimes. With the temperature dropping approximately three degrees per thousand feet in altitude, it doesn't take long to break out the cold weather gear.

The same group as appeared on page 82 appears here. They got tired of seeing Paul sleep on the ramp.

BEECHJET 400A

We flew to the Orlando area and met Tom Reilly at his warbird restoration museum, Tom Reilly Vintage Aircraft, based at Kissimmee Airport. A television crew from the Wichita CBS affiliate came along to produce a story about me. John Odegard of Raytheon and I agreed that it would be positive exposure for general aviation and specifically for the Beechjet 400A.

We spent two days dodging storms as we proceeded to Key West, then back up to central Florida. Our perseverance paid off. The brochure shoot was successful, and so was the television spot, which was picked-up nationally and nominated for a regional Emmy. It was also fun for my children to see what I do for a living.

Left to right: Pilot Roy Lawrence, Pilot Ed Berger, Pilot Tom Reilly, Copilot Loren Peters, Photographer/Assistant Tom Jenkins, Paul, Manager Media and Promotions John Odegard, Account Executive Tom Bertels, News Photographer Doug Schrag, and TV Aviation Reporter Bryce Matteson

CITATION I & II

This was one of my earlier shoots with the TallMantz B-25. They actually had two planes in service at John Wayne Airport in southern California. It was a wonderful education to sit around and listen to Frank Pine tell stories of filming movies like *Catch 22, The Great Waldo Pepper* and *It's a Mad, Mad, Mad, Mad World*.

Frank insisted that I keep my harness attached at all times while in the tail. I had no problem with that, but he was fanatical that I tell him when I was traversing from the tail (therefore unattached) to the mid-plane position. It wasn't until years later that I heard about a movie cameraman falling from the tail during the filming of *Catch 22*. Now I use two harnesses at all times.

Left to right: Assistant Jim Meyer, Paul, Pilot Bob Fizer, Cameraman Patrick Allen, Advertising Manager Rand Mickulecky, Advertising Director Ralph Aceti, Film Director Fred Ashman, Pilot Walt Pine, Pilot Frank Pine, Mechanic Wayne Burtt, Pilot Morgan Lilly, Pilot Mike Mahurter, Pilot Mike Tiller, Pilot Sam Wilson, Account Executive Jon Zimmerman, Art Director Peter deBoer, and Copywriter Tom Bartholomew

CITATION S/II

Don and Nancy Brinton have been involved in advertising general aviation airplanes for decades. Don's designing talents have allowed him to work with numerous aviation related corporations. When Cessna introduced the Citation S/II, Don and I worked together on the elaborate product brochure. We landed at NAS Alameda across from the San Francisco skyline and waited for sunset. The next day we flew to the Grand Canyon and captured the striking blue mountain shot.

Left to right: Tom Zwemke, Nancy and Don Brinton. Mary Ann Van Sickle who provided the models for an airplane boarding shot, is seen in the middle of the group. Her husband Bud is standing second from the right.

CITATION V

Felix prepares to enter the optionally equipped extra wide door. The company has ordered an Excel to replace the V. Felix's cargo includes gear and AT&T personnel.

Felix Macguire was born in Ireland and through a long, varied piloting career, landed in Anchorage, Alaska. I met him while covering an article on how Alascom (AT&T) used its Citation V. I spent three days with him and rode along as he made his rounds throughout the state. We picked up and dropped off cargo and personnel. In one day we covered most of the state with four stops. It's interesting to see corporate aircraft used so diversely to save time and effort. Those of us actively involved in aviation realize that business jets are *not* toys or perks for corporate officers. They can become some of the most efficient tools in a company's arsenal.

Felix divides his time and love between his wife Agnes and their children and grandchildren, his aviating, and his parish. As an ordained Catholic Deacon, he has the responsibility of performing every spiritual function allocated to an ordained priest. He is sincerely devoted to his congregation. He clearly represents the quality of people I have consistently met in aviation. It's an honor to call him a close family friend.

SINO
SWEARINGEN

Ed Swearingen is an aviation icon. His name has appeared on numerous airplanes. Most recently, he created the sleek and speedy SJ30-2. Sino Swearingen is currently seeking certification of this lovely light jet. Ed surrounds himself with people of quality. His quiver is filled with ex-Raytheon notables; Jack Braly, and two close friends of mine for many years, Chester Schickling and Mike Potts.

Left to right. Paul, Director Corporate Communications Mike Potts, Test Pilot Carroll Beeler, Vice President Quality Assurance Bob Homan, and Pilot/Lead Ground Support Engineer Phil Livingston

4

PROPJETS

King Air C90B

Assuming the position, left to right: Lori Hildreth, Whitney Hildreth, Dr. Jennifer Sullivan, Paul, Meghan Sullivan, Gail, Dennis Hildreth, Earlene and Bill Condiff, and Blair Sullivan

This shoot took place in southern Florida during the week between Christmas and the New Year. Gail came along to assist me and the pilots and client brought their spouses, a small compensation for working over the holidays. We always work long hours, starting early and ending late into the evening. But on most assignments, there is some down time during the middle of the day. This translated into beach time.

However, one of the days was not so leisurely. After a morning session, we scheduled an afternoon flight to Bimini Island, due east from Ft. Lauderdale. We departed in the Baron with the doors removed, Gail seated beside me. We were in the lead as we passed low over the Island. After circling a few times without landing we headed for a sunset of the Miami skyline. That accomplished, in the dark, windy, and cold Baron, we continued to our base in Naples on Florida's west coast. After landing, we were approached by two plainclothes Drug Enforcement Agents who questioned us about our low flying activities in an airplane without doors. Just when we had them convinced that we were on a photo mission, we heard the Black Hawk helicopter land. Out jumped fully armed troops in black garb, ready for action. I'm sure they were disappointed when they discovered the only drugs we were interested in were a couple of well earned drinks.

KING AIR B200

Fred George has been part of my life for many years. As senior editor at *Business* and *Commercial Aviation* magazine, Fred flies airplanes provided by the manufacturers and reports his findings. With all of the general aviation activity in Wichita, I see Fred often.

On this occasion, we got to play with the King Air B200. This airplane has been around a long time. Raytheon keeps making improvements without altering the parts that have made the King Airs the most successful line of propjets ever produced.

KING AIR 350

The images on these two pages represent two different photo sessions, one for aerials, the other specifically for ground shots. When producing an ad series or brochure, the art director sometimes provides a comprehensive layout, a COMP, for the photographer to follow. Other times, we head out and take a shotgun approach, amassing as much variety as possible, and building a brochure. Usually, it's a combination of both techniques.

ABOVE: Left to right: Pilot Walt Pine, Art Director Mike Dennis, Pilot Blair Sullivan, Advertising Director Ron Crotty, Photographer/Assistant Dick Yauk, Pilot Steve Mead, Pilot Kevin Eldridge, Mechanic Mike McDougall, and Paul

PICTURED TO THE LEFT: Left to right: Art Director Jim Gampper, Carefree SkyRanch Airport Manager Frank Lougee, Account Executive Tom Bertels, Photographer/Assistant Tom Jenkins, Pilot Ken Mikolajchak, Pilot Ed Berger, and Paul

STARSHIP

The Starship is one of the most fascinating airplanes I've ever photographed, and it is unmistakably a Burt Rutan design. I was first introduced to the Starship when I went to Burt's "Skunk Works" in Mojave, California. We shot the 80% proof-of-concept model from the B-25. Imagine what that must have looked like from the ground as we flew over.

Through the years I have had many opportunities to capture this semi-stealth creation on film. It is great to photograph because its personality changes with slight angle, lighting, or lens changes. Most planes have one or two visual personalities, but the Starship has many.

The shot with the XKE was for *Flying* magazine. The Starship belongs to Raytheon. But, more importantly, the Jag belongs to Jack Braly.

Left to right on the ground: Advertising Director Ron Crotty, Photographer/Assistant Dick yauk, Account Executive Steve Fushelberger, Pilot Tom Carr, Pilot Mark Carter (took the B-25 photo that appears on the back cover of this book), Alan Power, and Paul. Linda Liscom and husband Ed Power are in the nose of the B-25, and Pilots Walt Pine, Kevin Eldridge and Mark Foster occupy the cockpit area.

Mark II (JPATS)

Left to right standing: Pilot Tom Carr, Bob Laymon, Pilot Ralph Royce, Pilot/Mechanic T.C. Jones, Pilot Steve Young, and Team Leader Erik Andersen
Kneeling: Photographer/Assistant Tom Jenkins, Pilot Bob Newsom, Pilot Mike Burke, Pilot Jack Seltman, and Paul

Raytheon was awarded the coveted JPATS military trainer contract. Prior to naming the recipient of the contract, all competitors produced literature to introduce the candidates. My assignment included ground and aerial shots. We shot from the B-25 based in Galveston at the Lone Star Flight Museum, from a 58 Baron with the doors removed, and from the cockpit of a second Mark II. This last platform was the most exciting.

Shooting aerials is always disorienting. After all these years, I still get slightly queasy after each flight. Few people can look through the lens while circling without becoming ill. I was a little anxious when I heard we were going up to fly 12 loops and 12 rolls - in formation as I shot through the canopy. I took two motion sickness pills and asked Tom Carr, my friend and experimental test pilot, to be gentle with me. He smiled, and went into the briefing, carefully pointing out the ejection seat handle located between my legs where my cameras rested.

"Never, never yank your cameras up quickly," Tom said. "They might be hooked to the ejection seat handle."

That got my attention. As we departed in the cramped quarters, I gained an increased respect for Tom as we danced through the sky in formation. The vertical shot pictured here was during one of the many loops. To my delight, and thanks to Tom's piloting, the only sensation I experienced during the flight was pure exhilaration.

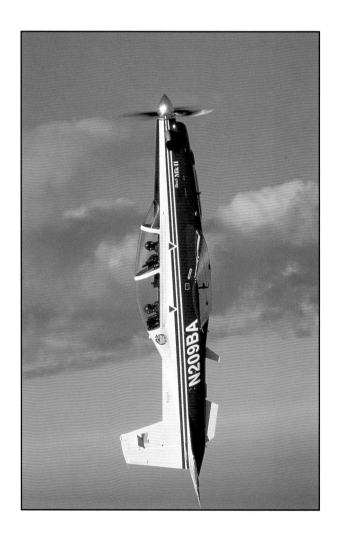

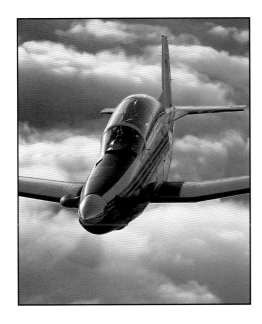
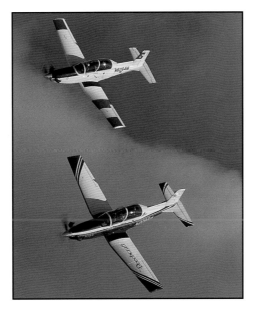

ERA AVIATION
DASH 8

Alaska is a great location to shoot in the summer. Sunset and sunrise light go on forever and the backdrops never quit.

Paul Landis at Era Aviation brought Gail and me to shoot a corporate brochure. Gail and I fell in love with Alaska and made lifelong friends.

PILATUS PC12

Cloud formations off the eastern coast of Florida provide some of the most beautiful backgrounds as the sun reflects off the ocean below. This gorgeous sunrise off Vero Beach led us toward the Gulf Stream.

Jessica Salerno at *BCA* magazine hired me to cover the PC12 for a pilot report. The large single engine propjet was easy to photograph. Bill Bubb flew the formation as we danced amongst the misty caverns.

PILATUS PC12

Chris and Pat Finnoff have been involved with general aviation forever. Their most recent venture is marketing the PC12 in North and South America. This excellent single engine propjet is built in Switzerland and its attention to detail reflects the Swiss obsession with quality.

This major assignment combined the needs for Pilatus product advertising with a day dedicated to shoot for *Flying* magazine. We headed west from Jefferson County Airport in the Denver area to begin shooting in California. We shot from a Cessna 210 and the Planes of Fame B-25, *Photo Fanny*. John Maloney piloted both platforms. I was treated with meeting the PC12 pilot Vaughn Olson and his wife Katie. As we got to know each other we revealed similar histories. Both of us surfed as we grew up in southern California. We both had lived and surfed near Santa Barbara during our college years. Other similarities helped solidify a camaraderie and kept us laughing throughout the week. His experience as a Marine aviator (or maybe it was his surfing) proved key to the success of the mission. Vaughn ranks among the top formation pilots with whom I have flown.

Standing left to right: Pilot/Mechanic Matt Nightengale, Pilot Jeff Titus, Pilot Steve Hinton, Pilot John Maloney, Pilot Vaughn Olson, Katie Olson, and Video Photographer for Jeppesen, Virgil Poleschook Kneeling are Tom and Paul

CHEYENNE IIIA

Meigs Field in Chicago has been the center of much controversy. Its proximity to the downtown business district makes it valuable property to corporate travelers. Unfortunately, it is also a valuable property to other interests. The battle over keeping Meigs open tugs at the heart of general aviation.

Left to right: Pilot and Advertising Director Earle Boyter, Photo Assistant Mike Newby, Model, Model, Paul, Pilot Chuck Bockstahler, Art Director David Pina, and Creative Director David Rushlow

PIAGGIO P180

Jim Kandt, then senior art director with Sullivan Higdon & Sink advertising agency, and I arrived in Genoa, Italy, to shoot ground and aerial shots for brochures and ads. Before we arrived, arrangements had been made for the aerial mission. Unfortunately, we were informed that the platform we would be shooting from would be a helicopter. We were further informed that we would hover, while the Avanti would fly by. We laughed, but were informed that to save face, we must shoot as arranged. We agreed, but insisted that a back-up plan be implemented. The helicopter shoot went as expected. Two days later we had a second chance, thanks to Dr. Ing. Feliciano Lasagni, our contact at Piaggio.

The Italian Air Force showed up with a C-130 and a pilot who spoke English. I was shuttled to the cargo door, strapped in, and off we went. After takeoff, my intercom went dead. In vain I kept yelling and signaling to the cargo crew that I couldn't talk with the pilot, who was the only English-speaking Italian aboard. How could I direct the target planes? The cargo crew kept smiling and giving me the thumbs up as I became more frustrated. Then they opened the HUGE cargo door in flight, and my heart went nuts. I must say that sitting out there, on the edge, by myself, made me reconsider shooting weddings. Fortunately, the gremlins fixed the intercom, and we lived to toast our success.

Paul and Art Director Jim Kandt salute the Italian Air Force for a most memorable excursion.

Piaggio P180

Flying magazine hired me to shoot the Avanti P-180 for a cover story. Coincidentally, the manufacturer had hired me to shoot advertising shots. To save time before a scheduled service requirement, we combined the shoots.

Fred George was the assigned editor covering the story for Flying. An extremely accomplished formation pilot and my buddy, Fred flew the P-180. After many years, Fred and I still reminisce over the great time we had, both while we were flying and while we swapped lies at the dinner table.

Left to right: Pilot Gary Beard, Pilot John Maloney, Pilot Steve Hinton, Pilot and Editor Fred George, Pilot/Mechanic John Hinton, Art Director Bryan Jessee, Cheryl Jessee, Photographer/Assistant Tom Jenkins, and Paul

CARAVAN

According to *Flying* magazine, the Cessna Caravan is the "DC-3 of the 1990s." It does everything. It can be found in jungles and the wintry north country. I've shot them in both places.

One February I got a call from Tom Zwemke at Cessna asking if I'd like to go to Pickle Lake, Ontario, Canada. I've always wanted to do some summer fishing in Canada, so there was no hesitation on my part. Then, he told me we were going the following week.

A few weeks later, Tom called again, this time assuring me the temperatures were to be more moderate. He had set up a shoot in Texas to simulate a military operation. When it came time for the group picture, we couldn't resist.

By the way, I'm still waiting for Zwemke's call to go to Tahiti.

ABOVE: Tom Zwemke and Bob Conover try to warm up.

BELOW: BUSTED! Pilot Mike Mahurter, Director of Corporate Communications Tom Zwemke, Video Cameramen David Wolf and David Drew, and a gang of still photographers "assume the position."

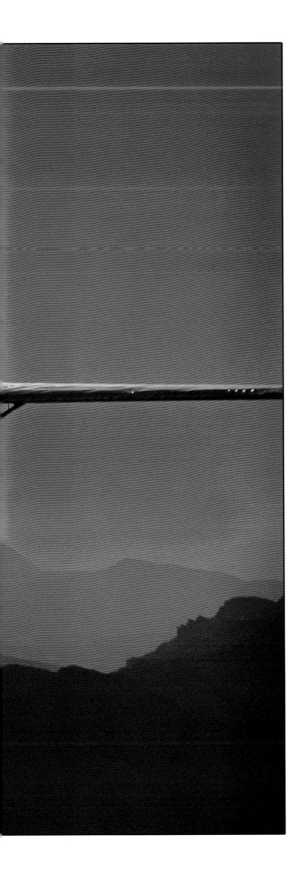

PISTON SINGLES AND TWINS

5

SKYHAWK

I shared the excitement of the reintroduction of the 172 Skyhawk and 182 Skylane with the entire general aviation community. Cessna had provided small single engine high-wing airplanes for training and introductory ownership for decades. Due to the product liability issue, production had ceased until Congress introduced a bill to limit manufacturer's legal responsibilities. Independence, Kansas, became the new production site for these extremely popular icons.

I was honored to be contacted to travel for a week shooting both planes in the western states. As we pulled into FBOs for fuel, small crowds would gather to inspect the revived models and reminisce.

Left to right: Paul, Tom, Pilot Rich Manor, Model Trudy Bastman, Model Mike Valletta, and Art Director Rick Kaufman
Not pictured: Pilots Kirby Ortega and Greg Pavlish

Skylane

The Cessna 182 Skylane is a fine airplane, substantial, dependable, and now nicely trimmed out. The redesigned interior rivals an expensive twin. We took the Skylane to the west coast looking for a variety of backgrounds. We weren't disappointed. I first shot the full line of Cessna singles in the early 1970s. It's fun to be shooting them again.

Skylane RG

I've taken pictures of Cessnas since 1972. When my cousin's husband, Randy Wittman, told me he had a 182 with retractable landing gear at John Wayne Airport, it was a natural that we arrange for an aerial photo session. I called my buddy Fred George and asked if he'd like to go play in the air for a while. He flew his Mooney up from San Diego, and we briefed for a sunset shoot.

After introductions and a safety briefing, we took off and headed for Santa Catalina Island. We shot from another Cessna with the window raised. As we manuevered around the island, the sun cast striking relfections and patterns on the Pacific. Don't tell my clients, but I have so much fun shooting, that sometimes I do it just for fun.

Copilot Fred George and Pilot Randy Wittman fly in tight formation with the platform camera plane

BONANZA

The Bonanza is a classic airplane. It is built beautifully and looks great. It feels substantial when you take the controls.

Gail assisted me and secured models and props when we took the A-36 and a 58 Baron to Jackson, Wyoming. We've worked for years with the crew that was on this shoot. There's nothing like working with a professional crew. We walked away with unique shots and warm memories.

Paul, Tom, Model Frank Vann, Mother of child models, Model, Gail, Model on wing, Pilot Ed Berger, Account Executive Tom Bertels, and Art Director Jim Gampper

BARON

The Grand Teton Mountains in Jackson Hole are uniquely identifiable. Within the restricted airspace, we flew around the range, hardly able to take a bad picture. The clouds and fog added an interesting element as we passed near Yellowstone National Park.

My very first aerial location shoot was of a Baron, shot in this area. Pilots Gary Brigham and Dave Palay introduced me to excellent formation flying. Mike Piper was my contact in the advertising department at Beech. He was along on my first local Wichita aerial shoot, also of a Baron. That was my first and last encounter with airsickness. It was Mike who kept hiring me, and started the aerial portion of my career. His boss, Jim Yarnell, was responsible for Beech's excellent advertising. An excellent photographer himself, I'm pleased that Jim is my senior by enough years that he's not my competitor today.

Left to right: Director of Public Relations Mike Potts, Paul, Gail, Pilot Ed Berger, Account Executive Tom Bertels, Assistant Tom Jenkins and Art Director Jim Gampper.
Background: George, Tommy, Teddy, and Abe

COMMANDER

When we landed in northern New Mexico, it was a lovely day. Clean, high altitude air greeted us. After some "touch and goes," we bundled up for a cool evening aerial session. We continued the session into Colorado and over to Lake Powell.

It was great to be working with Dean Thomas again. Dean and I logged many aerial hours together when he was with Piper. Now he was in charge of advertising for Commander. I was reminded how small the aviation community is and enjoyed the bonus of being able to rekindle old friendships.

Left to right top row: Photographer/Assistant Tom Jenkins, Pilot Walter Murphy, Pilot Harvey Kautz, and Pilot John LeGrand
Standing left to right: Senior Vice President Marketing and Sales Commander Aircraft, Dean Thomas, Pilot and owner Barry Aviation, Tim Barry, Tim Barry, Jr., Sean Barry, German Pilot Andre Schnarrenberger, and Paul

ARCHER

I only remember this assignment by the photographs. I had pneumonia during the shoot. I'd been in Delaware shooting Westwinds when I became ill. Double pneumonia, 103° temperature and deliriousness. I was supposed to leave immediately for Florida to meet with the Piper crew. My close friend Earle Boyter understood my condition, but because of all the pre-production clearances with the Bahamian government, he encouraged me to try to continue with the planned shoot. He laughed and said that they'd strap me into my seat so that if I collapsed I wouldn't fall out of the plane. After a day's rest, I agreed, and the following five days remain a blur.

The goal of the shoot was to capture four planes with textured backgrounds. My favorite was the Archer, because of the red paint scheme. While basing out of Spanish Wells Island, we came across this DC-3 for the group shot. Legend has it that it made a low pass over the island to land and drop off an undefined cargo when it was surprised by DEA agents. An aborted landing was followed by an aerial chase in the night. As the DC-3 circled the island, it dropped "square grouper" bails of vegetation until it ran out of fuel. A belly landing in the bay ended when the plane came to rest where we photographed it. The crew and cargo disappeared into the night.

Left to right: Paul, Dean Thomas, Joe Ponte, Earle Boyter and Art Director Andi Arnovitz from Fahlgren, Swink, Nucifora Advertising Agency

WARRIOR

Mark Twombly has written for numerous aviation publications. An assignment for *Flight Training* magazine teamed us up in Florida for a sunset series with this Warrior. The magazine has a unique inside front-cover photograph that is the complete reversal of the outside-front cover. This makes the photo session more of a challenge than a normal shoot. Mark is an excellent writer and editor, and he handles the controls of an airplane like the pro he is. Most pilots who don't fly close formation regularly aren't able to put the subject plane where I request. Mark proved the exception. I like the guy, and I respect his writing and flying.

Mark Twombly flies formation from the copilot's seat.

MALIBU

The Piper Malibu is a sleek, fabulous airplane. When I first met the designer, Jim Griswald, he showed me the test model I was about to shoot. I walked around the plane and commented: "This one is different. This is special." And it was.

Years later I found myself shooting the new Malibu Mirage while traversing Oregon. My longtime friend Earle Boyter had scheduled the shoot with Art Director David Rushlow. This was one of the last major projects we worked on together before Piper went through so many changes in the 1990s.

You have to land and fuel somewhere - It might as well be Aspen. Left to right: Paul, Earle Boyter, Andy Cendric, David, Phil and Lee Rushlow of Group 3hree Advertising

SENECA V

On January 16, 1997, The New Piper Aircraft Company revealed its Seneca V to a small group of aviation writers and select friends and employees. Mac McClellan, editor in chief of *Flying* magazine, was scheduled to be the first writer/pilot to fly it for a "pilot report" article and a sunrise photo session.

We had gone to bed the previous night, lulled to sleep by a driving rain. At 5:00 a.m., the Weather Channel reported a tornado watch north of Vero Beach. A 6:00 a.m. briefing at the airport revealed a break in the storms. We headed east over the Atlantic and got on top at 6,000 feet. Flying with cooperative and highly qualified formation pilots turned a potential "washout" into these striking images.

Left to right: Jeff Krell, Jim Duncan, Bart Jones, Mac McClellan, and Paul

KATANA

The sunrise shot of the Katana over Lake Powell is one of my favorites. I like the airplane, and I love the lighting and background. I used a graduated filter to enhance and darken the sky. I love shooting at the lake.

We worked our way through Sedona, Monument Valley, and all the special scenery in Arizona. Ed and Jeanine Helmick, local Arizona residents and fanatical off-road Jeep explorers, were our guides and Cessna 206 platform pilots. Jeff Owen flew the Katana, but he missed all the sights because he flew tight formation.

Left to right: Jeff Owen, Ed and Jeanine Helmick, and Paul

KATANA

I love to use clouds and water as backgrounds, because they are constantly changing. I try to enhance the scene through filters.

We were working out of Diamond Aviation FBO in San Carlos, California, when we ventured into San Francisco to capture the evening shot. I used my Canon EOS-1n 35mm camera, Kodak E100SW slide film, a 30CC magenta filter over a 28-70mm zoom lens. Then I lit the Katana with the Canon Speedlite 540EZ hand strobe for fill flash. It sounds pretty technical, but the Canon made it relatively simple.

Jeff Owen and Paul fly around the pattern. Paul used a wide-angle lens to capture this shot.

MOONEY

Left to right: Showing off the strength of the Mooney wing are Mooney President Jacques Esculier, Pilot Jeff Dunbar, Pilot Clay Wilcox, and Pilot Morris "Skeeter" Berry

Fernandez Bay Village Resort, Cat Island, Bahamas

Left to right: Jeff Dunbar, Dirk VanderZee, Paul and Clay Wilcox

What a great trip this was. We started in the northeast during the changing of the leaves. The weather was marginal, but we grabbed a few fine images. Fortunately, the "powers that be" suggested we head for the Bahamas for variation of backgrounds. No convincing was necessary on my part.

We toured the Bahamas for a few days chasing clouds and islands. Eventually, the clock struck midnight, and I had to return to Wichita.

MOONEY

Herman Dyal, partner and art director at fd & s design and communication (aka Fuller, Dyal & Stamper) arranged to shoot a gaggle of Mooneys in southwestern Texas.

We spent the night as guests of Dr. John Barnett at his Livermore Ranch retreat in the hills near Alpine, Texas.

Left to right standing: Herman Dyal, Ranch Staff Lynn and Brian Calhoun, Brian's mother Betty Calhoun, Dr. John Barnett, Mooney President Dirk VanderZee, and Ranch Foreman Tad Vernor
Kneeling: Pilots Clay Wilcox, Morris "Skeeter" Berry, and Rick Pitner
Missing from photo: Randy Keith, pilot of red plane over clouds

6

SPORT PLANES AND MORE

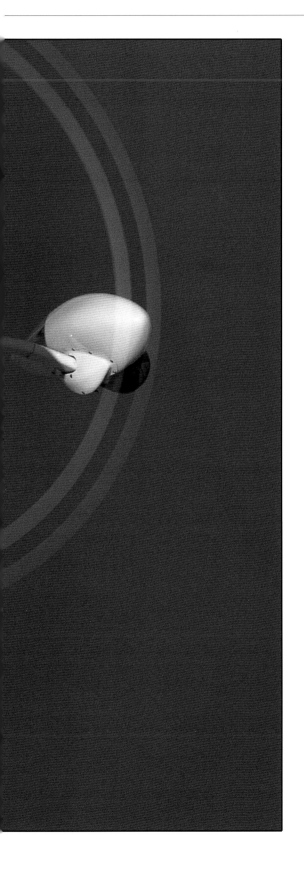

PATTY WAGSTAFF

Gail and I met Patty at the annual FBO judging sponsored by Murray Smith at *Professional Pilot* magazine. Patty and I were judges and honored as "pilot of the year" and "aviation photographer of the year." Patty, Gail, and I became instant friends. I had an opportunity to fly with Patty a few months later at Oshkosh. It was great to be treated to my own mini air show.

Patty's aviation accomplishments are incredibly impressive including three consecutive titles as U.S. National Aerobatics Champion - competing against both men and women. Patty has retired from competition, but you can catch her performing as a regular touring air shows around the world.

Patty's autobiography, *Fire and Air*, is a gripping story of determination as you ride the emotional roller coaster of her life.

Patty flashes her contagious smile as she prepares for the flight

OSHKOSH

When I shot Patty Wagstaff at Oshkosh, she brought some friends along for the ride. I was fortunate enough to have a few minutes with legends from the air show circuit: Gene Soucy, Julie Clark, Sean Tucker, Bill "Burner" Beardsley, and Wayne Handley. I shot from Sean Tucker's Cherokee with the side, back doors removed.

DOOLITTLE RAIDERS

In 1994 I was honored to participate in the final gathering of the Doolittle Raiders to pay tribute to the passing of General Doolittle. We met in Van Nuys at Petersen Aviation for a briefing. Carl Scholl of Aero Traders fame in Chino, led the pilot briefing. We amassed seven B-25s to fly up the coast to Pebble Beach, drop flowers in the ocean near the General's home, then pass by San Francisco and land in Fresno for a hangar party. Twenty-five of the 34 surviving Raiders gathered in Fresno for the final assembly of the group.

Carl Scholl presides over the pilot briefing. It is always important to have a thorough briefing before flying formation. When you introduce this many airplanes and pilots who have never flown together before, it is critical that everyone understands the plan.

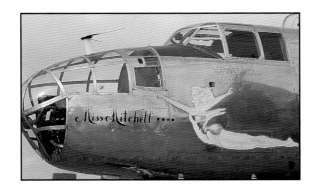

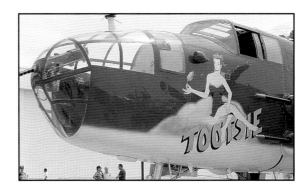

MUSTANG

Crazy Horse is a TF-51 that Lee Lauderback uses for training and pleasure flights. Many pilots have spent the day in ground school with Lee then taken to the skies to live out a fantasy in this dual controlled airplane. Mounted video cameras record the flight. Lee has experience in military fighters, helicopters, and corporate jets. When I first met Lee, he was Arnold Palmer's chief pilot. Stallion 51 is the corporation that owns *Crazy Horse*. It's a quality operation run by quality people.

Lee and son Brad fly together as often as possible. Here they fly low level over a Florida lake as they form up tight on the B-25.

MIG-17

Doug Shultz teamed up with us one evening when we were shooting Lee Lauderback in *Crazy Horse*. We caught a few images of the MIG, but due to its low fuel load, the session was brief. Doug did a great job slow-flying with us as I shot from the tail end of *Chapter 11*, the B-25 based in northern Florida.

SAAD WALLAN

I must admit that when Ed Parrish told me that Tom Jenkins and I were going with him to Saudi Arabia to cover an article for *Directions* magazine, I had very mixed emotions.

Of course, I wanted to experience new cultures and meet new people. Of course, I loved to travel and get paid while I scouted possible vacation destinations. But, Saudi Arabia? Well, was I wrong. I had a great time in Riyadh, and made a lifelong friend of Saad Wallan.

As I mentioned in the introduction, Saad has many business ventures, including the largest car dealerships in Saudi Arabia. But, most importantly, he loves his two sons and three daughters and is a most gracious host. I have come to learn that his hospitality and warmth are very common to the region. Although I couldn't begin to understand his culture in merely five days, I left Saudi Arabia knowing I had made a new friend and knowing my preconceived ideas of Saad's country were in error.

Tom Jenkins and Ed Parrish visit the historical sights in Riyadh with host Bandar Wallan, General Manager of The Qualified Advertising Co.

CAPTAIN
ROLIM AMARO

Brazil is a land of contrasts. Before my first visit, I only pictured the country as the Amazon Jungle and the beaches of Rio de Janeiro. I had no idea of the huge land mass, the modern city of Sao Paulo, or the warmth of the people.

Capt. Rolim Amaro typifies the genuineness of the locals. He owns numerous businesses including Taxi Aero Marilia S.A., the Cessna aircraft sales representative in Brazil. Although he is an extremely successful businessman, when I think of Rolim, his smile, the sparkle in his eyes, and his sense of humor immediately come to mind.

Rolim spends time on the weekends at his ranch located inland from his main businesses in Sao Paulo. His cattle and award winning horses have many acres to enjoy. There is even a landing strip located near the main ranch house.

CITATION SPECIAL OLYMPICS AIRLIFT

Cessna Chariman and CEO Russ Meyer is a visionary. He is well known and respected within the aviation industry and global business market, but his mark is felt way beyond financial reports. His legacy has found its place into hearts.

Russ conceived and, with the assistance of Airlift Director Marilyn Richwine, implemented the Cessna Citation Special Olympics Airlift. Certainly Russ and Marilyn would quickly add that it took hundreds of other individuals and corporations who contributed their time, talents and resources to make the airlift run smoothly. Citations, pilots and fuel were donated to transport athletes to the game site. I was able to fly with one group representing Kansas. When we landed, the athletes were thrilled with the flight, and the pilots had tears in their eyes.

I have always respected Russ, as a businessman, leader, and the head of a wonderful family. But now my respect has been raised to a much higher level. The world needs more business heroes like Russ Meyer.

AMERICAN BLIMP

How much fun can a guy have and still get paid? I had just finished three days of shooting a Gulfstream V from the B-25, when I hooked up with Jud Brandreth of American Blimp. We scheduled some aerials to be shot from an MD500 as we maneuvered around the blimp. My mind had to change gears to anticipate what moves I wanted the blimp to do to set up the shot. It's tough to climb on board a crowded commercial flight home after spending a week like this.

Vice President of Marketing Jud Brandreth and Paul try to warm up after a cool morning session.

EXECUTIVE AIRCRAFT CORP.

These two pages are dedicated to the memory of Stan Roth. Stan and his brother Jim were killed in an aviation accident on July 18, 1998.

Stan had gained a reputation for purchasing and selling high-end corporate aircraft. Over the years his Challenger fleet has rivaled most third world countries' air forces. Based in Wichita, Kansas, his FBO is located at Mid-Continent Airport. EAC periodically provides airplanes for me to use on the cover of *A/C FLYER* magazine. Managing Editor/ Editorial Designer Mike Perry used both these dusk shots as covers.

My eyes fill with tears and I choke on my words as I write this copy and have the printers reprint these pages. I found out about this tragedy as I was reviewing the final printed pages, ready to give my OK to have the book bound. I had great respect for Stan's business savvy. His little boy smile and twinkle in his eyes made you instantly like him. My wife, Gail, and I can't express how we feel for his wife Jan and their two sons. This is a sad day for me - a personal loss and a loss to the aviation community.

President/CEO Stan Roth, Chief Operating Officer Phil Jossi, and Aircraft Sales Agent Lloyd Curtis take their position on the stairs
Ground level left to right: Corporate Jet Sales Cliff Eldred, Sales Administrator Jennifer Brace, Scheduler Terri McKown, Special Projects Coordinator Terri Headrick, Customer Service Chris Peters, Aircraft Sales Agent Ken Stultz, Administrative Assistant Jan Moody, Advertising Coordinator Kara Miller, and Vice President Harry Littleton

DUNCAN AVIATION

When I think of Robert Duncan, I don't think of the businessman, I think of Robert Duncan, patron of the arts. Located in Lincoln, Nebraska, Duncan Aviation has become a destination for corporate aircraft sales and service. The quality and attention to detail found there is no accident. Duncan's involvement in the arts obviously influences his daily business.

Al Eidson of Eidson & Partners advertising agency worked with me on these photos. It's so stimulating to work for an agency and a client who appreciate something beyond the ordinary.

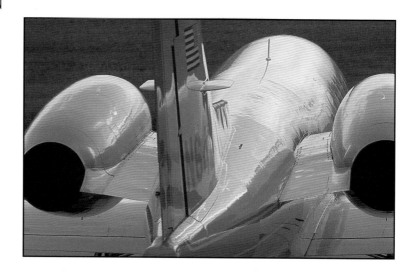

TIGERMOTH

Sid and Karen Tucker love airplanes and have owned many. Sid is director of the Citation FlightSafety International training facility in Wichita. In their spare time, Sid and Karen tinker around with their airplanes, and sometimes even fly them. I captured them together in the Tigermoth over El Dorado Lake.

Karen and Sid prepare for the evening aerial session.

PITTS
SUPER STINKER

The Pitts Super Stinker came to Wichita for a short time. I had a great time shooting with Ed Saurenman and Mark Knoll. Ed's father, Leo, flew his Cessna 180 as we shot close formation. Ed's competitive aerobatic background made my shooting easy. These two are a great father-son team.

Leo, Mark, Ed, and Paul stand in front of a Meyers 210 "Spirit" before a flight

7

HELICOPTERS

APACHE LONGBOW

What can I say about this machine? What a wild shoot for someone accustomed to photographing business airplanes. The British government was investigating various helicopters to purchase in bulk. Promotional materials were needed, so a video crew from Europe and I were hired. The ground shots were taken in Mesa, Arizona. We then headed for Orlando to hook up with Martin Marietta and shoot some aerials. The time allotted for aerials was limited, and the Jet Ranger helicopter we shot from was shared between both filming crews. With elbows flying, all photo requirements were met. A few months later, the McDonnell Douglas and Westland Helicopters partnership was awarded the contract for equipment and maintenance.

The ground shots were taken in Mesa, Arizona. Scenes were staged with military personnel positioning themselves around the Apache.

The action photography was shot in Orlando, Florida. Air-to-air and air-to-ground were shot on video and stills. The scene above, right, shows the video crew as they direct the aircraft by radio. The video monitor is protected under the dark cloth.

Left to right: Cameraman Graham Berry, Director Martin Denning, Producer Brian Creese, and Project Director Julian Browne

ROBINSON R22

Scott Spangler, editor of *Flight Training* magazine, needed cover shots for an article about tail rotors. The magazine uses a "reverse" photo on the inside cover, which mirrors the front cover. These two dusk images were used. I used 1,000 watt quartz lights on the rotor and studio strobes on the side of the Robinson R22. A long exposure allowed me to balance the ambient light.

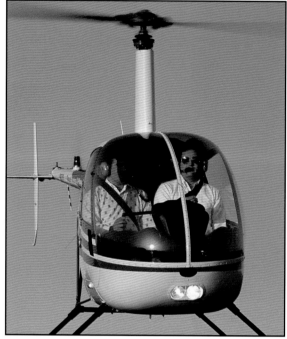

Pilots Emil Schreiber and James Rose make low passes by the camera.

JET RANGER

Mac McClellan, editor in chief of *Flying* magazine, called me and asked if I wanted to visit Texas, low level. We met at the Bell factory near DFW Airport, and off we went. The Dallas skyline offered us the business background we hoped to find. The clouds reflected in the buildings were a bonus.

SCHWEIZER 330

I met Barbara Tweedt at a helicopter convention in Miami. I showed her my portfolio, and we became instant friends. A few years later I traveled to the company headquarters in rural New York and shot a session for Schweizer.

Elmira, New York, is located in a hilly area in the Finger Lake region. Pilots Cole Hedden and Dave Savage treated me to a low level aerial ballet as we danced by trees, hills and lakes. What a fun way to be a tourist.

SCHWEIZER 300CB

I returned to Elmira to shoot the newly revamped trainer, the 300CB. These photos would be used for advertising by Schweizer, and for an article in *Flight Training* magazine. Scott Spangler, editor of the magazine, arranged for a joint shoot. It worked out beautifully as we took advantage of the fall foliage.

AGUSTA

Agusta helicopters are unmistakably of Italian design. Using the Miami skyline as a backdrop, we hovered at sunrise. Moving toward the Florida Keys rewarded us with a completely different background. Steve Fushelberger coordinated the advertising shoots for Agusta. It's always nice to work with efficient professionals who become close friends.

Steve Fushelberger stands by the nose of this Siai Marchetti S-211 based at Marathon, Florida. Next to Steve is Agusta Technician Andy Dnovaro, Pilot Dennis Tierney, Pilot Larry Graves and Marchetti Owner Steve Mair

192

ERA AVIATION HELICOPTERS

Paul positions himself on an oil rig near Anchorage. Special flight suits must be worn in case you must ditch in the frigid water. The bright color aids in search and rescue.

I spent nearly two weeks in the Anchorage, Alaska, area shooting for Era Aviation. The equipment Era flies includes Dash-8 and Twin Otter commuters, Learjet and King Air medical airlift planes, and various helicopters used in all imaginable ways.

Bryan Blixhavn runs the rotary-wing side of Era. Helicopters are perfect for "Flightseeing Tours" around glaciers, fire fighting, aeromedical transport and shuttling workers and gear to offshore oil platforms. What a great experience to land on one of those platforms. Because of the severe weather conditions in Alaska, the pilots and passengers must wear survival clothing, even in the summer, in case they go down in the cold water.

On a personal note, my friends Dave and Barb Anderson were returning to Alaska from a missionary flight to Russia, when the twin engine airplane they were in went down. All passengers survived in the cold water by clinging to empty gas cans which had been in the airplane. They were rescued by an Era Aviation helicopter crew before hypothermia set in.

8

PANELS AND INTERIORS

BOEING

Collins avionics products can be found on almost anything that flies. Christina deWolf is an art director and friend with whom I have worked on various accounts: Beech Aircraft, Piper Aircraft and Collins. When she called me to go shoot a Boeing 747-400 and 767 panel in Seattle, I packed immediately. She decided to add colored filters on our lights to help distinguish between the panels. The shoot was even more enjoyable thanks to the fresh seafood that evening.

Sometimes "real people" are used, instead of models, for the pictures - Pilot Client, copilot Art Director Christina deWolf. Paul and Tom are always just Paul and Tom.

CESSNA

Cessna manufactures the widest range of general aviation airplanes. The reintroduction of the Skyhawk 172 allows aviators to purchase a new high-wing Cessna with modern avionics as standard equipment. At the other end of Cessna's product line, in a category by itself, stands the speedy Citation X. Most airliners would love to have this panel. Jeff Filby and Rick Kaufman, both art directors at Sullivan Higdon & Sink advertising agency were responsible for the finished products.

HAWKER

John Odegard at Raytheon called me to shoot the Hawker 800XP interior. I was looking forward to this job. I knew the Hawker would be a nice airplane, and it was large enough so I would have room to move around with my camera and tripod. After spending a few days shooting, I wondered what it would cost for Raytheon to redo the inside of my van.

GLOBAL EXPRESS

What an incredible airplane! I had read about its speed and range, but I couldn't appreciate the spacious luxury until I entered it. The lavatory was as large as my room in college. Obviously, all interiors for this category airplane are custom designed.

Shooting an airplane of this size provides unique challenges. Airplane availability became a concern. Then the sheer size makes it difficult to set up all the lights. And when I was shooting the "talent," that's photographer talk for models, I had to use a bull horn so that those in the back could hear my direction. Even with all the difficulties, I would still take an airplane in trade for my invoice. I'm still waiting for Steve Phillips, director of advertising and promotions at Bombardier Aerospace Business Aircraft, to present me with the keys. I'm afraid it may be a long wait!

This large group includes: Director of Advertising and Promotions at Bombardier Aerospace Business Aircraft Steve Phillips, Creative Director Larry Dionne, Models Andrea Webb-Watson, Matthew O'Toole, Dan Carroll, Stylist Gail Bowen, Marketing Promotions Coordinator Christina Ryan, Models Susan Fay, Will Shaw, Richard Wilson, Richard Seaver, Victor Syng, Photographer Dan Russell, and Paul

Not shown: Models Rhonda Husak, Assistants Brian Cozine, and Tom Jenkins

GALLERY

MAGAZINES

Over the years I have worked with many aviation magazines. These next six pages are a sampling of over 400 cover photos with which I've been credited. As I've said before, there is a large team behind the scenes that made these covers possible.

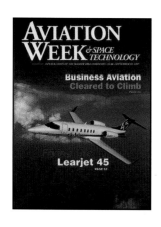

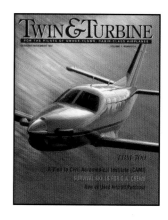

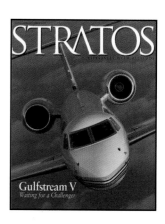

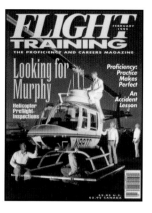
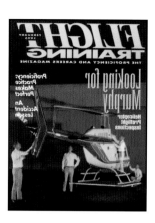

BCA AND A/C FLYER

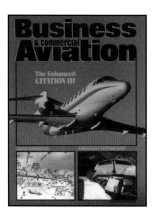

I have worked closely with Jessica Salerno, managing editor of *BCA*, for nearly ten years. I have a close friendship with her and her husband Jim Swickard.

A/C FLYER allows me complete artistic freedom in shooting its covers. Mike Perry, managing editor, art directs the *A/C FLYER* covers from New York while discussing ideas with me over the phone. We've worked together for years talking nearly weekly, but we've never met in person.

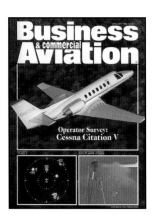
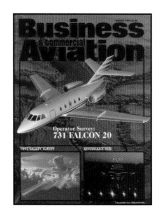

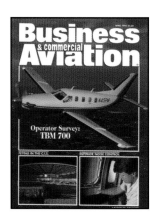

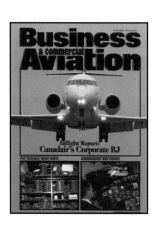
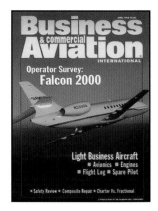

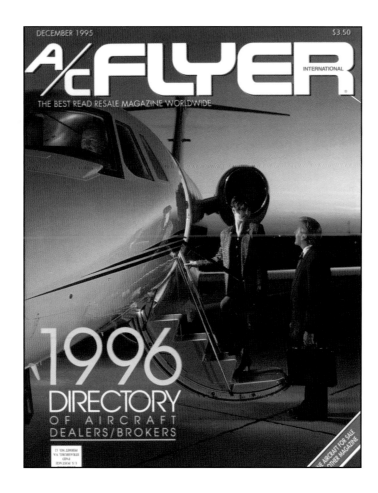

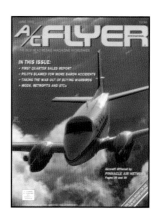

FLYING MAGAZINE

My first *Flying* magazine cover was in 1982. Since then, I have worked with many great writers: Dick Collins, Bill Garvey, Nigel Moll, Tom Bennenson, Fred George, and the current Editor in Chief Mac McClellan. These guys have influenced more young pilots than history will tell.

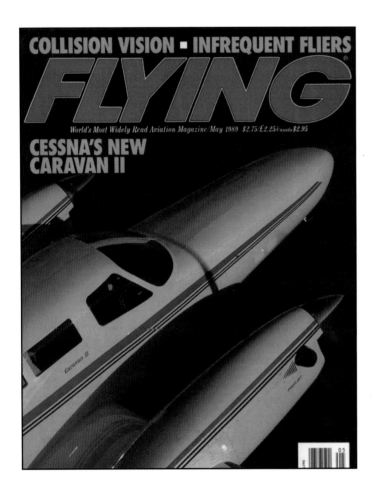

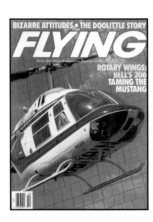

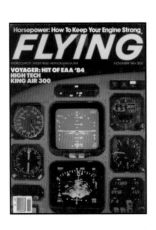

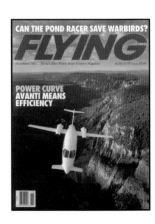

HOW TO KNOW WHEN IT'S SAFE TO TAKE OFF

FLYING

November 1994

World's Most Widely Read Aviation Magazine

CITATION ULTRA
More performance than expected

AIRPLANES OF THE FUTURE

USED ARROW REPORT

RECORD-SETTING TRIP IN A LEARJET 31A

Cessna Single Turns Propjet: An In-Flight Report

FLYING

DECEMBER 1992

World's Most Widely Read Aviation Magazine

Tips on Procedures and Rules of Ice-Flying

Fanjet or Turbojet? Two Learjets Tell the Story

WHY IS A MOONEY MSE BETTER THAN A 201?

FLYING

World's Most Widely Read Aviation Magazine

MORGAN RECALLS VIETNAM FLIGHTS

LOW-COST GPS FROM GARMIN

HOW TO GET THE MOST FROM A GALLON OF FUEL

FLYING

December 1994

PC-12: THE BIGGEST SINGLE

HUGH DOWNS HAS CLOSE CALL IN TIGER MOTH

TIPS FOR WINTER FLYING

USED DEBONAIR IS A BEST BUY

HOW TO AVOID **WIND SHEAR**

WILL LIGHTNING STRIKE YOUR AIRPLANE?

FLYING

World's Most Widely Read Aviation Magazine April 1991

SOVIETS SELL MINI BEARCAT

SHOOTING AIR-TO-AIR

COMING OF AGE: CITATION III

Technique: Aerobatics for Confidence and Skill

FLYING

FEBRUARY 1992

World's Most Widely Read Aviation Magazine

305 KNOTS AT FL310
Mike Smith's Snappy Turbine Single

Low Level Wind Shear: A High Level Problem

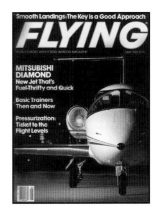

Smooth Landings: The Key is a Good Approach

FLYING

MAY 1992

World's Most Widely Read Aviation Magazine

MITSUBISHI DIAMOND
New Jet That's Fuel-Thrifty and Quick

Basic Trainers Then and Now

Pressurization: Ticket to the Flight Levels

TEN BEST USED SINGLE-ENGINE AIRPLANES

FLYING

April 1992

World's Most Widely Read Aviation Magazine

BEST USED BUY IN THE SKY IS 182

THE REAL LIFE OF LEARJET TEST PILOTS

WHERE DO THOSE EXPENSIVE AD NOTES COME FROM?

Corkey Fornof: The Boy Raised With a Bearcat

FLYING

World's Most Widely Read Aviation Magazine

Self-Evaluation: Are You Prepared for the Unexpected?

Enduring Skylane Top Big Single Choice

OSHKOSH FLIGHT PLAN ■ KNOWING YOUR LIMITS

FLYING

World's Most Widely Read Aviation Magazine/August 1988 $2.50

STUART MILLAR: THE CUB IS BACK!

FAA WRITTENS PUT TO THE TEST

NONPRECISION APPROACHES ■ SOUND EFFECTS

FLYING

World's Most Widely Read Aviation Magazine

AIRLINE PILOT PREP SCHOOL

THE NEW WAVE OF TURBINE SINGLES

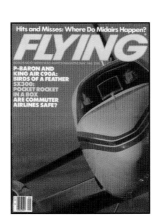

Hits and Misses: Where Do Midairs Happen?

FLYING

World's Most Widely Read Aviation Magazine/May 1992

P-BARON AND KING AIR C90A: BIRDS OF A FEATHER

SX300: POCKET ROCKET IN A BOX

ARE COMMUTER AIRLINES SAFE?

KLN 90B: GPS APPROACHES WITH A MOVING MAP

FLYING

World's Most Widely Read Aviation Magazine

BFR FACE-OFF
Our experts check each other

WHY IFR PILOTS LOSE CONTROL

WORLD-RECORD CLIMBING
Gulfstream rewrites the book

Used Skyhawk Review

MAGAZINE ADS

I have worked with some outstanding advertising agencies and art directors. Photography is an important element in the final ad, but the layout, use of type, and copy create the total package.

1. McCann Erickson - Art Director Bob Sullivan
2. Fotouhi, Alonzo, Cameron - Art Director Tony Huelette
3. Fotouhi, Alonzo, Cameron - Art Director Tony Huelette
4. Camstra Communications - Art Director Chuck Edelman
5. Marketel - Art Director Steve Crawford
6. Leo Burnett - Art Director Jim McComb
7. Boyd Kleypas & Assoc. - Art Director Mark Weldon
8. Keetin, Rich & Dickerson - Art Director Orlando Castro, Account Executive Ron Jackson
9. Ingalls Advertising - Art Director Jim Kandt
10. McCann Erickson - Art Directors Jesse Caesar and Mike Dennis
11. McCann Erickson - Art Director Jesse Caesar
12. Sullivan Higdon & Sink - Art Director Jeff Filby
13. Sullivan Higdon & Sink - Art Director Jeff Filby
14. Sullivan Higdon & Sink - Art Director Rick Kaufman
15. Sullivan Higdon & Sink - Art Director Jeff Filby
16. Sullivan Higdon & Sink - Art Director John Bacon
17. Sullivan Higdon & Sink - Art Director Rick Kaufman
18. Sullivan Higdon & Sink - Art Director Jeff Filby

1

2

3

4

5

6

7

8

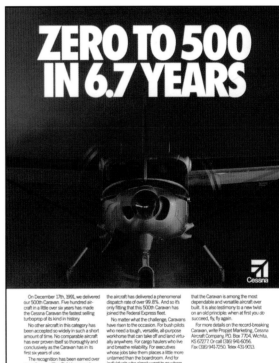

Magazine Ads

1

2

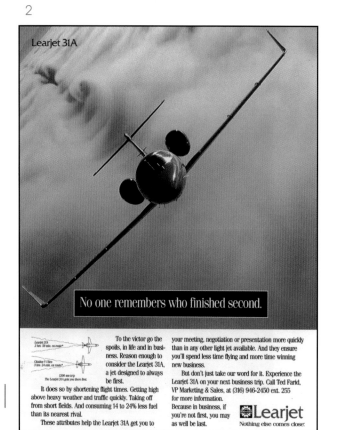

3

4

5

216

6

7

10

8

9

11

12

13

14

15

16

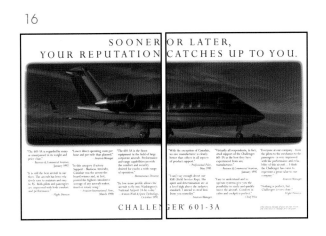

POSTERS

Over the years there have been many requests for images to hang on the wall. We have a series of posters, fine art original photographs, and fold-over note cards. Shown here are some of the 24 x 30 inch posters currently available. For more information or a catalog, please call 1(800)697-2580.

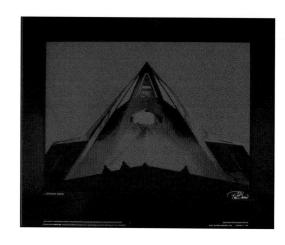

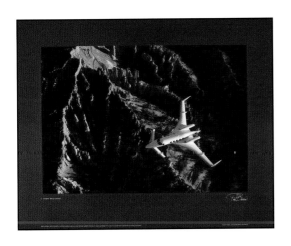

Outtakes

1

1. Doug Farrar, account executive, and Ingrid Sepahpur, art director, at Bailey Lauermen & Assoc. advertising agency, Gail, Tom, Ann Stuever, Aubree Bowen, Evan Senn, Heather Smith, Dan Peare; seated, Paul and Tony Marlow, director of marketing, at Raytheon TravelAir
2. Ed Berger is all style
3. Tourist Fred "the nerd" George, helping Paul and family with directions to the beach
4. Model, Paul McClean, is caught relaxing
5. Ben Budzowski with a low pass in the CitationJet Photo: Jeff Filby
6. The Starship photo crew at the Nut Tree Airport
7. Art Director Jeff Filby
8. Ed Parrish in hot water again
9. Princess Sharon Core being tended to
10. Mac McClellan and Pete Reynolds practicing their formation pointing
11. Tony Marlow and John Odegard
12. Ed Berger and Roy Lawrence
13. Paul and Fred George
14. Oops!
15. John Ross in rare form
16. Paul and brother Lance returning from Hawaii, 1962
17. Betcha' can't find Bob Brown and Ed Berger
18. Paul and brother Lance on Maui, 1997

2

3

4

5

6

7

8

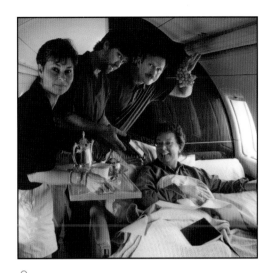

9

10

11

12

14

15

13

16

17

18

Outtakes

1. Aubree and Evan sneak a taste, as their "parents" nap
2. This really is Paul. circa 1970
3. Gail is dressed for a party, but unknowingly strikes a familiar pose. circa 1993
4. Paul is caught relaxing
5. Tom and Paul - Photo by Garth Dingman
6. More formation pointing: Paul, Dick Yauk and Tom
7. Major turbulence
8. Tom is preparing for a high-altitude shoot in an experimental Learjet
9. Gail is hoisted by the Raytheon and B-25 gang: Paul, John Maloney, Matt Nightengale, Roy Lawrence, Greg McCurley, Randy Rosebrock, Steve Hinton. and Craig Holderman oversees from above
10. Ashley is lifted by Beechjet crew: Paul, Garvin Speed, Ron Crotty, Tom, Roy Lawrence, and Steve Mead
11. Tom and Debbie
12. Gail and Paul
13. Some of Paul and Gail's High School Sunday School Class redecorating: Shawn, Jes, Shawn, Jennifer, Gail, Selena, Lisa, and Paul
14. Golfer Dylan Senn practices his putting
15. Photographer Garth Dingman
16. Aubree, Evan, and Dylan
17. Aubree, Paul, and Ashley
18. The Bowen crew in trouble again: Paul, Ashley, Gail, Dylan, Aubree, Evan and Chloé the dog

1

2

3

4

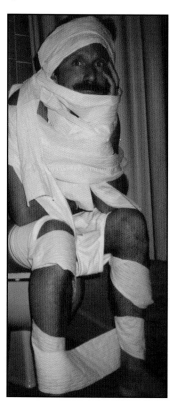

5

6

7

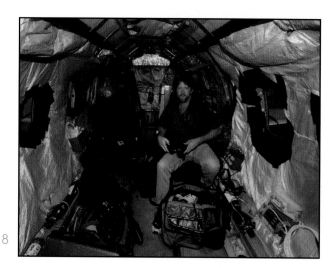

8

9

10

11

12

13

14

15

16

17

18

ACKNOWLEDGMENTS

There are some people who have not been mentioned in the book, but have made behind-the-scene contributions to it and to my life. This is my opportunity to say, "Thank you."

In the dedication I spoke of my life's partner, Gail. Some of the main reasons I love her and married her in 1993, were the commitment, tenderness, and loving discipline she shared with me for the other two most important people in my life - my daughters, Ashley and Aubree. My girls and I are extremely close. Ashley is studying business communications at the University of Kansas. This past summer she was an intern with Public Relations Director Dave Franson at Learjet while also earning her private pilots license. Aubree is in middle school and has chosen from her many talents and interests to become a veterinarian.

As a bonus to our marriage, Gail brought two stepsons into my home - Dylan, and Evan, who is pictured at the right. She also brought a wonderful Christian family; her parents Don and Imogene Hilton, sisters Dawn, Julie and Ann, and nine nieces and nephews.

Certainly I appreciate my parents, Lance and Cora Bowen. I thank them for their part in contributing to who I am today. I wish my father could have seen this book before he died in 1996 after retiring from McDonnell Douglas Aerospace. I gained an early appreciation for airplanes because my uncle, Ralph Gibbons, and my father introduced my brother, Lance, and me to their beauty and mystique. I developed a love for aviation and I identify it with some of the best times in my life.

I grew up in southern California. Many of my parents' friends, including Tom and Helene Woods, became my friends. Bruce and Roland Lagareta, Dr. Steve Johnson, Mike Grimes, and Pat Laughlin, were school, neighborhood, and surfing buddies. Mike died in Vietnam. I sporadically keep in touch with the others and we always pick up where we left off.

Rev. Don Williams, pastor to college students at the large First Presbyterian Church of Hollywood, developed programs for the "street people" of the 1960s. Included were free meals, crash pads, drug, emotional, and spiritual counseling, a coffee house with live music, and friendship. I helped by taking photographs and playing keyboard in a folk-rock band and a jazz group. Out of that time came my friendships with Brian and Janis Hahn, David and Sharon Covington, Pam, Tim, and the entire Van Valin family, Cobina Beaudette, Dr. R. B. "Biff" and Pam Oliver, John Block, Bob Marlow, and Bob Papazian.

I moved to Wichita in 1971, and made new friends centered around the halfway house I directed and the aviation industry. Through the halfway house, I met Doris Akin, Bill Mah, Pete and Elanore Amstutz, Tom Rozof, Ralph Teran, and Robin Wilborn. One of my first friends in aviation was Dave Franson, then at Cessna. Similarly, my friendship with Steve Millham at Beech/Raytheon has lasted over two decades. Dean Humphrey, retired Cessna PR director, remains one of my favorite people.

When I became a professional photographer in 1973, I lived in the country adjacent to the home of Norman and Pat Lee. Their daughters, Nancy Lee and Kathy Lee Vickers, became the younger sisters I'd never had.

As my career developed, I worked with *Flying* magazine's staff; Dick Koening, Pat Luebke, Hilary Lawrence, Nancy Bink, and Russ Munson, whose photography I admire greatly. My out-of-town friends include Martha Pine (Frank Pine's widow) and her sister Ruth "Boots" Tallman (Frank Tallman's widow), Graham Jackson (deceased), Dick Aarons, Bob Sullivan and Photographer George Hall. Local aviation friends include Jan McIntyre, Dave Pishko, Frank Mitchell, Dave Carter, Bailess Bell, Brian Barents, Al Higdon, Charlie Geer, and Tom Schiller. Strong non-aviation relationships flourished; Michael Phipps, Terry Green, Jim Bunck, Cheryl Alley, Carina Michel, Rondy Merlau, George Charlsen, Mick Hilleary, Greg Sullivan, Leesa Walker, Brent Ward, Pat Collins, Matt All, Jim Reed, Dr. Doug Nielsen, Bernie Barge, and Creative Director Sonia Greteman.

I met and married Lynda Hastings in 1976. In all fairness, credit for the early photographs in this book must be shared with her. She encouraged me during my early years of photography and shared in the creation of my two wonderful daughters. I enjoy continued closeness with her parents, Aubrey and Roberta Hastings. Through Lynda I met Rich and Donna Roberts and David and Sharen Haines - four great people. Kent Kruske's friendship and business expertise have been invaluable. Over the years, as she cared for the girls, Elva Schouten became an additional "grandma."

When Gail and I married I inherited another set of friends. Doctors Rick and Kim Hartwell, Wayne and Norma Roberts, Bob and Deanna Liebl, and Wade and Juliana Kloefkorn. Gail inherited my friends too, including Jim Healey in Monte Carlo.

As our children grew, their friends became our friends; Tonya, Tammy, Teresa, Brooke, Josh, Brett, Scott, and Joey. Gail and I treasure the time with the high schoolers in the Sunday school class that we jointly teach. The sharing, honest questions, and friendship mean a lot to us. They challenge us to be real. And, they remind me that friendship has no age barriers. Thanks for accepting our friendship unconditionally: Shannon, Selena, Shawn, Joy, Jennifer, Shilo, Shon, Becky, Karen, Don, Kristen, Lisa, Mike, and Josh.